Lead with Purpose or Be Led by Circumstance

The New Rules of Leadership in a World That Won't Stand Still

Douglas B Sims, PhD

DB Sims, PhD

Lead with Purpose

Table of Contents

Acknowledgments

I am deeply grateful to my wife for her unwavering support, wisdom, and the incredible journey of love and partnership we've shared for over 34 years. Your presence has been my foundation, my guiding light, and a constant source of inspiration in life and throughout this process.

To our two children—you have filled our lives with immeasurable joy, challenges, and lessons that continue to shape and enrich us. Watching you grow has been one of life's greatest privileges, and your experiences have been both a source of pride and a reminder of the ever-evolving nature of learning and leadership.

To our family—thank you for walking this path with us. Your love, encouragement, and unwavering support have been a bedrock of strength along the way.

I also extend my sincere appreciation to my friends and colleagues. Your insights, experiences, and shared moments have been invaluable in shaping this book. The conversations we've had, the lessons we've exchanged, and the perspectives you've offered have added depth and real-world relevance to these pages. Your openness and contributions have been indispensable, and I am truly grateful.

Finally, to the many individuals I have quietly observed in malls, theaters, and everyday life—you, too, have played a role in this journey. Your interactions, behaviors, and unspoken lessons have provided fascinating insights that have enriched my understanding of human nature. Thank you for being an unwitting yet essential part of this exploration.

Forward

Leadership is not what it used to be. The days of rigid hierarchies, command-and-control management, and leadership by title alone are long gone. Today's world demands a new kind of leader—one who is adaptable, decisive, and able to navigate a landscape of rapid change, uncertainty, and complexity.

The 21st century has thrown every traditional leadership model into upheaval. The rise of remote work, generational shifts in the workforce, artificial intelligence, and global disruptions have rewritten the rulebook on how organizations function. Those who cling to outdated leadership styles—who insist on leading the way it's always been done—risk irrelevance, failure, or worse, becoming the bottleneck to progress.

That is why this book, Lead with Purpose or Be Led by Circumstance, is not just timely, it is essential. Douglas Sims, PhD doesn't sugarcoat leadership. He doesn't peddle the tired clichés of "inspiring vision" or "leading with passion" without substance. Instead, he delivers a clear, no-nonsense framework for thriving as a leader in today's world. Whether you're an executive, a mid-level manager, or an ambitious professional looking to step up, this book lays out the real, unfiltered truths about what it takes to lead effectively now and into the future.

Dr. Sims has founded and built five corporations, ranging from micro-businesses to large national firms with locations across six states. Not only did he successfully negotiate the sale of these companies for substantial profits, but this experience also refined his leadership abilities, enabling him to create and sustain successful organizations. This expertise ultimately paved the way for his transition from industry to academia, where he became the Dean of a School of Science, Engineering, and Mathematics.

What sets *Lead with Purpose or Be Led by Circumstance* apart is its focus on practicality. Dr. Sims masterfully distills decades of research, experience, and insight into actionable strategies—ones that leaders can apply immediately. From decision-making under pressure to fostering trust in an era of skepticism, from leading multi-generational teams to harnessing the power of adaptability, this book delivers a comprehensive blueprint for leadership success in the modern era.

Most importantly, this book compels readers to confront a fundamental truth: Leadership is a choice. You can either step up, evolve, and lead—or you can find yourself at the mercy of those who do. The question is not whether leadership is changing; it already has. The real question is: Will you lead, or will you be led?

If you're ready to take control of your leadership journey, to rise above outdated models, and to master the new rules of leadership, then turn the page. Your future as a leader starts now.

Chapter 1

Defining Solid and Impactful Leadership

In my early years of professional employment, I saw solid and failed leadership at all levels. Witnessing these two dichotomies provided me with a unique perspective on leadership—what to emulate and what to avoid. Great leadership drives innovation, inspires teams, and secures long-term success. But bad leadership? It breeds stagnation, low morale, and ultimate failure. From nepotism and poor hiring to a resistance to change, leadership missteps can cripple an organization.

This chapter unveils the core principles of effective leadership, exposes the pitfalls that sink organizations, and delivers actionable strategies to build a culture of excellence. The difference between success and failure starts at the top; will you *Lead with Purpose* or *Be Led by Circumstance*?

Characteristics of Effective Leaders

Effective leadership is more than just holding a position of power—it is about inspiring, adapting, and fostering an environment where employees feel motivated and supported. Great leaders do not simply delegate tasks; they set the tone for the organization, creating a culture of accountability, collaboration, and continuous improvement. They recognize that their success is tied to the success of their teams, and they take deliberate steps to ensure that employees are empowered to

1

perform at their best. Below are key traits that define strong and impactful leaders.

One of the most essential qualities of effective leadership is visionary thinking. Exceptional leaders set clear, achievable goals and communicate a compelling vision that aligns teams toward a shared purpose. Instead of merely reacting to the present, they anticipate future challenges and opportunities, ensuring long-term organizational success. A strong leader does not just tell employees what needs to be done, they inspire them to believe in a greater mission. By outlining a roadmap for growth and innovation, visionary leaders create a sense of direction and purpose that keeps their teams engaged and motivated.

Equally important is emotional intelligence, the ability to understand, regulate, and respond to emotions in a way that fosters productive relationships. Leadership is not just about strategies and numbers—it is deeply rooted in human connections. Emotionally intelligent leaders are self-aware, empathetic, and skilled at managing interpersonal dynamics. They recognize when employees need support, when conflicts require mediation, and how to communicate in ways that strengthen trust and morale. A leader with high emotional intelligence cultivates a culture of respect, openness, and collaboration, ensuring that employees feel valued and heard.

The defining trait of great leaders is accountability and integrity. Strong leaders take full responsibility for their decisions and actions, rather than shifting blame onto others. They lead by example, setting high ethical standards and consistently demonstrating the values they expect from their teams. Integrity is the backbone of effective leadership—without it, trust erodes, and organizational cohesion weakens. When leaders hold themselves accountable, they create an environment where honesty, reliability, and transparency become ingrained in the workplace culture. Employees are more likely to take ownership of their work and contribute meaningfully when they see their leaders practicing what they preach.

Another critical skill of an effective leader is hiring to win. A great leader understands that the strength of a team determines the success of an organization. Hiring decisions are not made based on personal comfort, loyalty, or favoritism, but rather on securing the most capable individuals for the job. Strong leaders seek out the best talent, people who bring expertise, innovation, and a commitment to excellence. They recognize that surrounding themselves with top performers strengthens the entire organization. In contrast, a failed leader hires personal career cheerleaders who prioritize pleasing the boss over producing results. These hires exist not to challenge or enhance the organization but to boost the leader's ego, creating a culture of blind loyalty rather than strategic effectiveness. This weakens accountability, undermines the credibility of leadership, and damages team morale, as employees quickly recognize when favoritism takes precedence over merit.

Finally, adaptability is crucial in an era of constant change. The best leaders recognize that uncertainty and disruption are inevitable, and rather than resisting change, they embrace it. They remain flexible, open-minded, and proactive in seeking innovative solutions to new challenges. Adaptable leaders encourage their teams to experiment, take calculated risks, and approach obstacles with a problem-solving mindset. Rather than panicking in the face of uncertainty, they remain composed and guide their organizations through transitions with confidence. By fostering a culture of resilience and agility, they ensure that their teams can thrive in any environment.

Effective leadership is not about asserting dominance or maintaining control, it is about inspiring people, making ethical decisions, and continuously evolving to meet the needs of an ever-changing world. Leaders who embody these traits cultivate workplaces where employees feel valued, engaged, and driven to contribute to a shared vision. As we explore leadership successes and failures throughout this book, we will see how these principles play out in real-world scenarios and how aspiring leaders can integrate them into their own leadership approach.

Lead with Purpose

Characteristics of Ineffective Leaders

Ineffective leaders create environments of confusion, low engagement, and inefficiency. Rather than fostering growth and stability, they introduce uncertainty and disarray, often without realizing the full extent of their impact. Many of these leaders fail to recognize their own shortcomings, doubling down on poor decisions instead of seeking constructive solutions. Their unwillingness to learn, adapt, or accept responsibility leads to stagnation, high turnover, and ultimately, organizational decline. Below are some of the most common traits of leaders who hinder progress rather than propel their teams forward.

One of the most detrimental traits of ineffective leadership is short-sighted thinking. Leaders who fail to take a long-term view of their organization's success often set vague, unrealistic, or inconsistent goals that leave teams feeling directionless. Instead of establishing sustainable strategies, they chase quick wins, prioritizing immediate results at the expense of future stability. This leads to a cycle of short-term fixes—band-aid solutions that temporarily mask deeper issues rather than addressing them at the root. Organizations led by such individuals may see short-lived success but ultimately struggle to maintain long-term growth and resilience.

Another common flaw is emotional detachment, which severely impacts team dynamics and workplace culture. Leadership is not just about strategy and execution; it is about people. When leaders ignore or mishandle emotions, they create disengaged workforces where employees feel undervalued and disconnected from the organization's mission. Leaders who lack emotional intelligence struggle to build strong relationships, failing to recognize the importance of motivation, recognition, and support in maintaining team morale. Over time, this detachment results in increased turnover, lower productivity, and a workplace culture that breeds resentment and dissatisfaction.

A particularly damaging trait of ineffective leaders is blame-shifting and hypocrisy. Rather than accepting responsibility for failures or setbacks, these leaders deflect accountability onto their teams, external circumstances, or even their predecessors. This creates a toxic culture of fear and distrust, where employees are hesitant to take initiative or voice concerns. Furthermore, leaders who do not uphold the standards they set for others quickly lose credibility. If a leader preaches integrity and accountability but fails to demonstrate these qualities themselves, their hypocrisy becomes evident, eroding trust within the organization. Employees quickly recognize when leadership operates under a double standard, which can lead to widespread disengagement and cynicism.

Finally, rigidity is a hallmark of failing leadership. In a rapidly changing world, adaptability is essential for success, yet many ineffective leaders resist change, clinging to outdated practices and fearing uncertainty. Whether due to arrogance, fear, or a lack of vision, leaders who refuse to evolve often drive their organizations into stagnation. The inability to pivot in response to industry shifts, technological advancements, or market demands places the organization at a competitive disadvantage. In times of crisis, rigid leaders panic rather than innovate, making reactionary decisions that further destabilize their teams. In contrast, effective leadership requires embracing change, encouraging creative problem-solving, and fostering an environment where innovation thrives.

Ultimately, ineffective leaders not only undermine their own credibility but also damage the productivity, morale, and long-term viability of the organizations they oversee. Their failure to think strategically, connect emotionally, accept responsibility, and adapt to change creates an unstable and demotivating environment. In the chapters ahead, we will explore how these leadership shortcomings have played out in real-world scenarios and discuss actionable strategies for avoiding these pitfalls.

The Role of Communication in Leadership

Communication is the bridge between leadership and execution. Even the most visionary leader will struggle if they cannot effectively convey their ideas, expectations, and vision to their teams. A leader's ability to communicate determines whether their organization operates with clarity and efficiency or falls into confusion and inefficiency. Strong communication builds trust, fosters collaboration, and ensures that everyone is aligned with the organization's mission. Without it, even the best strategies fail to gain traction.

However, while communication is key, it is not the sole ingredient of leadership. A leader who simply enjoys giving speeches, delivering inspiring messages, or holding endless meetings does not automatically qualify as an effective leader. Charisma and eloquence may capture attention, but they do not replace the ability to make tough decisions, guide a team through challenges, or execute a vision with precision.

At its core, communication in leadership is not just about transmitting information; it is about creating understanding, inspiring action, and fostering a culture of openness and engagement. But words without action ring hollow. A true leader doesn't just talk about vision, they build the roadmap, navigate obstacles, and ensure their team has the tools and direction to succeed. Effective leadership requires both communication and execution, and those who mistake public speaking ability for leadership risk prioritizing rhetoric over results.

Below are critical aspects of leadership communication that define success—but remember, great communication is only valuable when backed by decisive action and genuine leadership.

The Foundation of Trust

Transparency is one of the most fundamental elements of leadership communication. When leaders communicate openly, they build trust, credibility, and a sense of stability within their teams. Employees who feel informed and included are more likely to be engaged, motivated, and committed to the organization's goals. Conversely, when leaders withhold information, provide vague directives, or operate in secrecy, it creates uncertainty, suspicion, and disengagement.

However, communication alone is not enough. A leader's actions must align with their words. A leader who says one thing and does the complete opposite quickly loses the respect of their team. Empty promises, contradictions, and hypocrisy erode trust faster than silence ever could. Strong leaders understand that credibility is built through consistency, and when words and actions don't match, the result is a disengaged, disillusioned workforce that no longer believes in their leadership.

The Impact of Transparent Leadership

Leaders who prioritize transparency create environments where employees feel secure and valued. When employees understand company objectives, challenges, and changes, they are more likely to take ownership of their roles, contribute innovative ideas, and work toward common goals. Transparency eliminates the fear of the unknown and provides clarity, allowing teams to stay focused on execution rather than speculation.

But here's the thing, transparency isn't just a trendy leadership buzzword. It's a practice, not a proclamation. Too many leaders talk about being transparent without actually following through. They throw around phrases like "open communication" and "honest leadership," but when it comes time to make real decisions, they keep employees in the dark, sugarcoat problems, or selectively disclose information to maintain control. This isn't transparency, it's performative leadership.

True transparency requires consistency, honesty, and action. For example, consider a CEO who openly discusses the company's financial health, strategic direction, and upcoming challenges in quarterly meetings. This approach allows employees to see the bigger picture, understand their contributions, and trust that leadership is making informed decisions. On the other hand, a leader who remains silent during times of uncertainty or hides behind vague corporate jargon breeds fear and anxiety, leading to disengagement and potential turnover.

And let's be clear—this extends to hiring. Leaders cannot claim they value fairness, merit, and the best candidate for the job, only to turn around and hire their personal cheerleader instead of the most qualified person. Saying one thing and doing another erodes trust faster than anything else. If hiring decisions are made based on favoritism rather than competence, it sends a clear message that talent and hard work don't actually matter—only loyalty to the leader does. That's not leadership; that's self-serving management.

If leaders want to build trust and inspire their teams, they must practice transparency, not just preach it. It's not about sharing everything, it's about sharing what matters, being honest about challenges, and ensuring employees feel informed rather than blindsided. When transparency is embedded in an organization's culture, including in hiring decisions creates a workplace where people feel respected, engaged, and committed to a shared vision.

The Cost of a Leader Who Lacks Transparency

When leaders fail to be transparent, they create an environment of uncertainty, suspicion, and frustration. Instead of fostering collaboration and trust, they breed skepticism and disengagement. Employees are left to piece together fragmented information, navigate through corporate ambiguity, and constantly second-guess leadership decisions. The result? A workforce that operates out of fear and frustration rather than motivation and purpose.

Take, for example, a department head who claims to value open communication but routinely withholds critical information about organizational changes. Employees hear whispers of restructuring but receive no clear direction, leaving them anxious about their roles and futures. Rather than focusing on their work, they spend time speculating, worrying, or, worse, updating their résumés in preparation for the worst.

Or consider a manager who preaches fairness and accountability yet continuously promotes their inner circle, disregarding talent and experience. When employees see that merit takes a backseat to favoritism, they disengage. They stop striving for excellence because they realize effort and performance don't matter—only proximity to the leader does.

A lack of transparency isn't just frustrating; it's toxic. It erodes trust, fuels resentment, and ultimately leads to high turnover and low morale. Employees don't need to know every detail of executive decisions, but they do need honesty, clarity, and consistency. When leaders fail to provide these, they don't just lose credibility, they lose the team altogether.

Key Aspects of Transparent Communication

Transparency in leadership is not just about sharing information, it is about fostering trust, alignment, and accountability within an organization. Employees perform best when they feel informed, included, and confident in the direction of the company. When leaders communicate openly about goals, challenges, and expectations, they create an environment where employees can fully engage with their work and contribute to the organization's success. Conversely, a lack of transparency leads to uncertainty, disengagement, and a breakdown of trust.

To cultivate a transparent workplace, leaders must go beyond occasional updates and instead commit to consistent, honest, and clear communication. This means providing frequent updates, being honest about challenges, setting clear expectations, and fostering an open dialogue where feedback is valued. These key elements ensure that employees remain aligned with leadership, understand their roles, and feel empowered to contribute meaningfully. For example, here are some key points:

- Frequent Updates: Regularly communicating goals, updates, and company progress keeps employees informed and aligned with leadership.

- Honesty About Challenges: Leaders who acknowledge difficulties and involve their teams in problem-solving foster a sense of collective responsibility.

- Clarity in Expectations: Employees perform best when they understand what is expected of them. Clear communication eliminates misunderstandings and inefficiencies.

- Openness to Feedback: Encouraging dialogue rather than one-way communication helps employees feel heard and valued.

A transparent leader ensures that information is accessible, honest, and timely, allowing teams to work with confidence and direction.

The Power of Understanding

While communication often focuses on what is said, active listening is equally, if not more important in effective leadership. Leaders who listen as much as they speak create a culture of collaboration, innovation, and trust. They make employees feel valued, heard, and empowered, which fosters a workplace where ideas thrive, problems are solved proactively, and morale remains high.

In contrast, leaders who dominate conversations, ignore employee concerns, or dismiss feedback create frustration and disengagement. When employees feel their voices don't matter, they stop contributing, innovation stalls, and resentment builds. Over time, this leads to a toxic work environment where people disengage, productivity declines, and turnover increases. Worse yet, when leaders refuse to listen, they make uninformed decisions based on assumptions rather than reality, leading to costly mistakes that could have been avoided with genuine dialogue.

True leadership isn't just about speaking, it's about understanding. The best leaders don't just communicate their vision; they actively seek input, acknowledge different perspectives, and adjust their approach based on meaningful conversations. When leaders prioritize listening, they cultivate loyalty, boost engagement, and create a workplace where employees are fully invested in the organization's success.

The Difference Between Hearing and Listening

Many leaders assume they are listening when they are, in reality, simply waiting for their turn to speak. Worse, many mediocre leaders will ask for your opinion not because they value your input, but because they are checking a box—they've already made their decision and aren't truly open to alternative perspectives. Active listening goes beyond passively hearing words, it involves fully understanding, processing, and responding to what is being communicated. This means paying attention not just to what is said, but also to tone, body language, and unspoken concerns.

For example, an employee might express frustration over a new policy in a team meeting. A poor leader might nod absentmindedly or offer a generic response without further discussion, dismissing the feedback as an obligation fulfilled. An effective leader, however, would genuinely engage—asking follow-up questions, probing deeper to understand the root of the concern, and thoughtfully considering how to address the issue meaningfully. Leadership isn't about checking boxes; it's about building trust and fostering collaboration through real, intentional listening.

Why Active Listening Matters in Leadership

Effective leadership is not just about giving directives, it's about fostering meaningful connections with employees, understanding their challenges, and creating an environment where everyone feels heard. Active listening is one of the most powerful tools a leader can use to build trust, enhance collaboration, and drive engagement. When leaders take the time to truly listen—not just hear—they demonstrate respect for their team's perspectives, concerns, and ideas.

Leaders who prioritize active listening create stronger relationships, improve problem-solving, reduce workplace conflicts, and enhance employee engagement. In contrast, leaders who dismiss or overlook the concerns of their teams create an atmosphere of frustration and disengagement. By making listening an intentional and integral part of leadership, organizations can foster a culture of collaboration, innovation, and mutual respect. For instance, active leadership will:

- Build Stronger Relationships: Employees feel valued when leaders take the time to listen to their concerns and insights.

- Encourages Problem-Solving: Leaders who actively listen can identify underlying issues and collaborate on solutions more effectively.

- Reduces Conflict: Miscommunication is one of the primary sources of workplace conflict. By listening carefully, leaders can prevent misunderstandings before they escalate.

- Boosts Employee Engagement: People are more engaged and motivated when they feel heard and understood.

How to Practice Active Listening as a Leader

Active listening is more than just hearing words—it requires full engagement, thoughtful responses, and a commitment to understanding the speaker's perspective. Leaders who actively listen foster a workplace culture of trust, collaboration, and open communication. When employees feel truly heard, they are more likely to share insights, raise concerns, and contribute to meaningful discussions.

To practice active listening effectively, leaders must be intentional about their approach. This means eliminating distractions, asking clarifying questions, reflecting on what has been said, and responding in a way that demonstrates genuine understanding and interest. By adopting these habits, leaders can strengthen their relationships with employees, improve decision-making, and create a more engaged and motivated workforce. Effective communication starts with active listening. When engaging in a conversation, especially in leadership or professional settings, demonstrating that you are fully present and receptive can make a significant impact. Here are key strategies to enhance your listening skills and foster more meaningful interactions:

- Give Full Attention: Maintain eye contact, put away distractions, and focus entirely on the speaker.

- Ask Clarifying Questions: Encourage deeper discussion to fully understand concerns.

- Reflect and Summarize: Paraphrase what has been said to confirm understanding and demonstrate attentiveness.

- Provide Thoughtful Responses: Avoid dismissive remarks and show a genuine willingness to engage in meaningful dialogue.

By prioritizing active listening, leaders cultivate a culture of respect and collaboration, where employees feel empowered to share ideas and voice concerns.

Avoiding Confusing Communication

A common failing among weak leaders is communicating with innuendos, vague suggestions, and conflicting messages. This type of communication creates confusion, frustration, and inefficiency among teams. When employees are left guessing about their responsibilities, expected outcomes, or the company's direction, their ability to execute effectively is severely compromised.

Strong leaders understand that direct and clear expectations are the foundation of effective leadership. Instead of speaking in riddles or offering inconsistent guidance, they provide straightforward instructions that leave no room for misinterpretation. Employees should never have to wonder what a leader "really meant" or waste time decoding ambiguous messages.

Why Clarity Matters in Leadership Communication

Clear and direct communication is the foundation of effective leadership. When leaders articulate expectations, goals, and decisions with precision, they eliminate confusion, foster alignment, and ensure that their teams can execute tasks with confidence. On the other hand, vague instructions, conflicting messages, or ambiguous expectations lead to misunderstandings, inefficiencies, and workplace frustration.

A leader's ability to communicate with clarity impacts every aspect of an organization. It ensures that employees understand their roles, reduces errors, prevents unnecessary workplace drama, and cultivates a culture of accountability and respect. When employees know exactly what is expected of them and how their work contributes to the bigger picture, they can focus on achieving results rather than deciphering unclear directives. By prioritizing clarity, leaders create an environment where teams work efficiently, stay aligned with the organization's mission, and operate with a shared sense of purpose.

Clear and effective communication is one of the most powerful tools a leader can wield. It not only sets the foundation for operational success but also strengthens team dynamics and organizational culture. When leaders prioritize clarity in their messaging, they eliminate confusion, align their teams with key objectives, and foster a workplace built on trust and accountability. Here's how clear communication drives organizational success:

- Aligns the Team with the Organizational Mission: When employees clearly understand their roles and how their work contributes to broader goals, they can perform with confidence and direction.

- Eliminates Inefficiencies: Clear instructions and expectations minimize mistakes, reduce the need for repeated explanations, and ensure projects stay on track.

- Prevents Workplace Politics and Misinterpretation: Leaders who rely on vague statements or backdoor suggestions create environments where assumptions, rumors, and uncertainty thrive.

- Fosters Respect and Accountability: When leaders communicate expectations transparently, employees respect their leadership and are more likely to take ownership of their work.

How to Communicate with Clarity as a Leader

Clear communication is a hallmark of strong leadership. Leaders who communicate with precision and consistency eliminate confusion, reduce mistakes, and ensure their teams remain aligned with organizational goals. When expectations are vague or contradictory, employees waste time deciphering what is required rather than executing tasks efficiently. Miscommunication leads to frustration, inefficiencies, and diminished trust in leadership.

To communicate with clarity, leaders must be intentional in their approach. This means being direct and specific about goals, maintaining consistency in messaging across different channels, using simple and concise language to avoid misinterpretation, and confirming that their instructions have been understood. By prioritizing clear and effective communication, leaders empower their teams to work with confidence, accountability, and focus.

Miscommunication can lead to inefficiencies, frustration, and a lack of trust in leadership. To prevent this, leaders must be deliberate in how they convey information. Clear and intentional communication ensures that teams understand expectations, stay aligned with organizational goals, and operate with confidence. Here are key strategies to enhance clarity in leadership communication:

- Be Direct and Specific: Avoid vague statements and clearly define what needs to be accomplished.

- Ensure Consistency in Messaging: Contradictory messages create confusion; leaders should ensure their communication remains aligned across all platforms and interactions.

- Use Simple, Concise Language: Overcomplicating messages leads to misinterpretation; straightforward language ensures better comprehension.

- Confirm Understanding: Ask employees to repeat or summarize expectations to ensure alignment.

By prioritizing clarity over ambiguity, leaders set their teams up for success. Instead of leaving employees to navigate uncertainty, they empower them with the knowledge and confidence needed to execute their responsibilities effectively.

Communication is the lifeline of effective leadership. A leader who fails to communicate clearly or listen actively risks losing the trust and engagement of their teams. Transparency ensures that employees remain informed, aligned, and confident in leadership decisions, while active listening fosters a culture of respect, collaboration, and innovation. Equally important, leaders must communicate with clarity rather than innuendos or conflicting messages, ensuring that expectations are clearly defined and consistently reinforced.

Great leaders do not just deliver messages; they facilitate understanding, encourage dialogue, and create an environment where everyone feels heard and valued. By mastering these key aspects of communication, leaders can build stronger teams, make better decisions, and drive long-term success within their organizations.

The Importance of Empathy and Inclusion

Leadership is not just about making decisions; it is about understanding and empowering people. Empathy and inclusion are critical components of successful leadership:

- Empathy: Leaders who take the time to understand their employees' experiences and challenges create a workplace culture of belonging and motivation. Employees who feel valued are more engaged and committed to the organization's mission.

- Inclusive Leadership: Diversity of thought leads to stronger decision-making and innovation. Inclusive leaders recognize the strengths that come from different perspectives and create an environment where all voices are heard.

Case Studies of Leadership Failures

Leadership failures can have devastating consequences, not just for the individuals at the top, but for entire organizations, industries, and even governments. When leaders lack vision, fail to communicate effectively, resist accountability, or make self-serving decisions, the ripple effects can lead to financial collapse, loss of public trust, and organizational dysfunction.

By examining real-world examples of leadership failures, we can identify the common mistakes that undermine success and learn valuable lessons about what not to do. These case studies illustrate how poor decision-making, lack of adaptability, ethical lapses, and misguided priorities have led to significant downfalls—serving as cautionary tales for leaders at every level.

Case Study 1: Fall of a Corporate Giant – Enron Scandal

Few corporate failures in history are as infamous and instructive as the collapse of Enron, a company once hailed as an innovative leader in the energy sector. At its peak, Enron was considered a Wall Street darling, boasting rapid growth and skyrocketing stock prices. However, beneath the surface, the company was engaged in widespread financial deception.

The company's leadership, particularly CEO Jeffrey Skilling and Chairman Kenneth Lay, prioritized short-term stock gains over ethical business practices. They manipulated financial statements through fraudulent accounting techniques such as mark-to-market accounting, which allowed them to inflate revenue projections based on speculative future earnings rather than actual profits. This created an illusion of financial stability while, in reality, Enron was drowning in debt and liabilities.

A toxic culture of secrecy, arrogance, and unethical decision-making permeated the company. Employees were discouraged from questioning leadership, and whistleblowers were silenced or ignored. When leaders foster a culture where dishonesty is rewarded and ethical concerns are dismissed, disaster is inevitable.

The collapse of Enron in 2001, following the revelation of its fraudulent activities, led to one of the largest corporate bankruptcies in history, wiping out thousands of jobs, billions in shareholder value, and shaking public trust in corporate governance. The scandal also triggered legislative reforms, including the Sarbanes-Oxley Act, designed to enhance financial transparency and accountability in publicly traded companies.

This case highlights the consequences of poor accountability, lack of integrity, and a corporate culture that values profits over principles. Leadership that prioritizes deception over transparency ultimately destroys trust, credibility, and the very foundation of an organization.

Case Study 2: Collapse of Blockbuster – A Lesson in Complacency

Blockbuster was once a dominant force in the home entertainment industry, with thousands of locations worldwide and near-total control over the video rental market. However, its downfall remains one of the most striking examples of leadership failure due to complacency and resistance to change.

In the early 2000s, Netflix approached Blockbuster with an offer to sell their company for just $50 million. At the time, Netflix was a struggling mail-in DVD rental service, and Blockbuster's leadership—believing their brick-and-mortar model was untouchable—laughed off the offer.

This proved to be one of the most catastrophic business decisions in history.

Instead of recognizing the shift in consumer behavior and the potential of digital streaming, Blockbuster's leadership remained fixated on their outdated business model, relying on late fees and in-store rentals. As Netflix expanded into streaming, offering a more convenient and customer-friendly service, Blockbuster failed to innovate. By the time they attempted to launch their own streaming service in 2010, it was too late—Netflix had already solidified its dominance, and Blockbuster had lost its relevance.

Blockbuster's rigid mindset and refusal to adapt ultimately led to its downfall. The company filed for bankruptcy in 2010, leaving only a single nostalgic store in Bend, Oregon, as a reminder of what once was.

This case serves as a powerful warning about the dangers of complacency in leadership. Organizations that fail to anticipate industry shifts, listen to market trends, and embrace innovation risk being left behind. Leadership is about more than managing day-to-day operations—it requires the vision and courage to evolve before disruption makes change impossible.

Case Study 3: Political Leadership Disaster – Response to Hurricane Katrina

Natural disasters are a test of leadership at the highest levels, demanding quick thinking, effective coordination, and decisive action. The government's response to Hurricane Katrina in 2005 stands as a textbook example of crisis leadership failure, marked by miscommunication, delayed responses, and lack of preparedness at the federal, state, and local levels.

When Hurricane Katrina made landfall on August 29, 2005, it devastated New Orleans and surrounding areas, causing massive flooding, destruction, and loss of life. While the storm itself was a natural disaster, the ensuing humanitarian crisis was largely man-made, as poor leadership and bureaucratic failures compounded the catastrophe. Key Leadership Failures in the Katrina Response:

- Failure to Act Quickly: Despite days of warning, government agencies were slow to mobilize resources. The Federal Emergency Management Agency (FEMA) and local authorities failed to evacuate residents efficiently, leaving thousands stranded in desperate conditions.

- Breakdown in Communication: Miscommunication between federal, state, and local officials led to confusion and inaction. Conflicting reports about available aid, the condition of levees, and rescue efforts further delayed critical response measures.

- Lack of Accountability: Leaders at multiple levels failed to take responsibility for their roles in the crisis. FEMA Director Michael Brown was widely criticized for his lack of urgency and inability to coordinate relief efforts. His infamous response, "We're seeing good progress"—while thousands remained stranded in life-threatening conditions, became a symbol of leadership incompetence.

- Inadequate Preparation and Infrastructure Failures: Despite previous warnings about the vulnerability of New Orleans' levees, no serious efforts were made to reinforce them before the storm hit. When the levees broke, the flooding turned catastrophic, exposing years of neglect and poor planning.

The consequences of these failures were devastating: over 1,800 lives lost, hundreds of thousands displaced, and billions of dollars in damages. More than just a natural disaster, Hurricane Katrina became a case study in how leadership missteps can magnify the impact of a crisis, turning a challenging situation into a full-blown catastrophe.

This case underscores the importance of strong, decisive, and compassionate leadership in times of crisis. Leaders must be prepared for the unexpected, communicate effectively, and take responsibility for ensuring the safety and well-being of those they serve. A leader's failure to act in a timely and coordinated manner can mean the difference between resilience and disaster.

Lessons from Leadership Failures

Each of these case studies highlights a different aspect of failed leadership—whether it be ethical misconduct, resistance to change, or crisis mismanagement. The downfall of Enron demonstrates how a lack of accountability and integrity can lead to widespread destruction. Blockbuster's collapse is a cautionary tale about the dangers of complacency and failing to embrace innovation. And the response to Hurricane Katrina reveals how miscommunication, poor planning, and a lack of decisive leadership can turn a crisis into an even greater disaster.

Leadership is not about maintaining the status quoit, it is about making difficult decisions, adapting to change, and taking responsibility for outcomes. These failures serve as stark reminders that when leaders prioritize personal gain over ethical leadership, ignore market trends, or fail to act in moments of crisis, the consequences can be catastrophic.

As we move forward in this book, we will explore what effective leadership looks like, examining the qualities, strategies, and mindsets that set great leaders apart from those who fail. The lessons from these failures are invaluable, offering a roadmap for current and future leaders to avoid the pitfalls of their predecessors and build stronger, more resilient organizations.

Finally, leadership is not just a hat you were, a badge you show, or a position of authority is the driving force behind success or failure. True leaders inspire, innovate, and create environments where people and organizations can thrive. Those who communicate with clarity, foster inclusivity, and embrace change set the foundation for long-term growth and resilience. On the other hand, leadership failures, whether through poor decision-making, ethical blind spots, or an inability to adapt—can unravel even the most promising organizations.

As we continue exploring leadership failures across industries, this book will uncover the critical missteps that derail progress and, more importantly, provide actionable strategies to help leaders rise above them. The fate of an organization does not rest on luck or circumstance, it hinges on the strength, vision, and integrity of those leading it. Whether you are an aspiring leader or a seasoned executive, the lessons ahead will challenge you to refine your leadership approach and ensure that you are building, not breaking, the path to success.

Chapter 2

Common Pitfalls of Failed Leadership

Leadership is the driving force behind any organization's success or failure. Strong leaders inspire teams, drive innovation, and create sustainable growth. However, when leadership is flawed, the effects ripple through the entire organization, leading to dysfunction, low morale, and stagnation. Failed leadership is rarely the result of a single misstep—it often stems from deeply ingrained patterns of poor decision-making, mismanagement, and neglect of fundamental leadership principles. Trust me, I have made many mistakes as a leader, the key is learning from those mistake and not repeating them.

In this chapter, we will explore some of the most common pitfalls that lead to leadership failure, including nepotism, poor hiring practices, lack of accountability, and resistance to change. These issues not only erode trust and efficiency within an organization but also diminish its long-term viability. By examining these pitfalls, leaders can recognize and correct their own shortcomings before they cause irreversible damage.

A Shortcut to Organizational Decay

Nepotism, the practice of favoring family members, friends, or personal associates in hiring and promotions—is one of the most corrosive leadership failures. While it may seem harmless or even practical to bring in trusted individuals, especially in family-run businesses or small organizations, prioritizing personal relationships over qualifications and competence undermines organizational credibility, weakens performance, and breeds resentment among employees.

At its core, nepotism disrupts the principle of meritocracy, where positions and promotions should be awarded based on skills, experience, and contributions rather than personal connections. When leaders choose loyalty over ability, they create an environment where competency takes a backseat to favoritism, ultimately leading to poor decision-making, lack of accountability, and an erosion of employee morale. Instead of rewarding hard work and talent, nepotistic organizations discourage innovation, limit career growth for deserving employees, and send a clear message that success is determined by who you know rather than what you can do.

The damage caused by nepotism extends beyond internal operations; it also significantly harms an organization's reputation. When customers, investors, and business partners recognize that key roles are being filled based on personal relationships rather than expertise, confidence in the organization diminishes. Stakeholders may question the integrity of leadership decisions, suspect financial mismanagement, and perceive the company as unprofessional or untrustworthy. This tarnished reputation can have long-term consequences, making it difficult to attract top talent, secure partnerships, and maintain customer loyalty.

Moreover, nepotism often creates inefficiencies that weaken an organization's overall performance. When unqualified individuals are placed in decision-making roles, they may lack the critical skills and knowledge needed to drive innovation, manage teams effectively, or navigate complex challenges. This leads to poorly executed strategies, operational bottlenecks, and ultimately, financial losses. Competent employees may find themselves forced to correct mistakes made by underqualified leaders, further draining productivity and causing frustration. Over time, the organization becomes less competitive, less adaptable, and more vulnerable to external disruptions.

Perhaps the most toxic aspect of nepotism is the culture of entitlement and resentment it fosters within the workforce. Employees who witness undeserving individuals being promoted or favored simply because of personal connections feel undervalued and demotivated, leading to disengagement, higher turnover rates, and a lack of commitment to the company's goals. Why should employees go above and beyond when they know their efforts will not be rewarded? This erosion of morale kills innovation and teamwork, as employees withdraw from contributing their best efforts, knowing that their career growth is limited by an unfair system.

I have seen this firsthand in almost every organization I have worked for. Nepotism is not a rare issue, it is a pervasive problem that erodes companies from within, often under the radar until the damage is done. It was because of this pattern that, when I built my own company, I made it a strict rule never to hire a friend or family member. More importantly, I never hired someone simply because I liked them. Hiring should never be about personal comfort or familiarity—it should be about winning. The key to a successful organization is to ensure that every single person on the team is the best possible fit for the role, not just someone who is easy to get along with.

Ultimately, nepotism is a shortcut to organizational decay, a slow but inevitable downfall fueled by favoritism, incompetence, and declining morale. To build something truly great, leaders must put personal relationships aside and commit to hiring for talent, expertise, and results. By fostering a culture of fairness and rewarding competence over personal ties, organizations can maintain integrity, attract top talent, and ensure long-term success. Hiring to win is not just a philosophy, it is the foundation of a thriving, high-performing organization.

How Nepotism Undermines Organizations

Nepotism is one of the most insidious threats to organizational health, creating a ripple effect of dysfunction that weakens productivity, morale, and long-term success. While it may seem convenient for leaders to hire or promote friends, family members, or close associates, doing so at the expense of more qualified candidates erodes meritocracy, damages credibility, and stifles innovation. Organizations that prioritize personal relationships over competence often find themselves struggling with disengaged employees, poor decision-making, and a tarnished reputation.

One of the most immediate and damaging effects of nepotism is that it erodes meritocracy. When leadership positions are handed out based on personal connections rather than qualifications, hard-working and competent employees see their efforts overlooked in favor of less-qualified hires. This leads to a culture of frustration and resentment, where employees no longer feel motivated to strive for excellence because they recognize that performance alone will not guarantee advancement. Over time, this disengagement spreads throughout the organization, leading to a decline in productivity, increased turnover, and a loss of valuable talent. When employees believe promotions are based on favoritism rather than merit, they stop putting in their best efforts, which ultimately weakens the organization from within.

Beyond internal consequences, nepotism damages an organization's external credibility. Investors, customers, and industry partners expect businesses to operate based on performance, innovation, and ethical decision-making. When favoritism is evident in leadership, it signals to external stakeholders that the organization values personal relationships over professional excellence, leading to diminished trust and reputational harm. Investors may hesitate to provide funding, customers may take their business elsewhere, and high-quality candidates may avoid applying for positions, recognizing that their careers could be stalled by an unfair system. A company's reputation is one of its most valuable assets, and when that reputation is tainted by nepotism, rebuilding credibility becomes an uphill battle.

Perhaps the most dangerous long-term effect of nepotism is that it weakens performance and stifles innovation. Leadership roles require critical thinking, problem-solving, and strategic decision-making, all of which demand a certain level of expertise and experience. When unqualified individuals are placed in key positions simply because of personal connections, the quality of decision-making deteriorates. These leaders often lack the necessary skills to navigate complex business challenges, leading to costly mistakes, operational inefficiencies, and poor strategic planning. Additionally, nepotism discourages creative problem-solving and fresh ideas, as those in power may prioritize loyalty and obedience over innovation and independent thinking. Over time, this stagnation leaves the organization vulnerable to competitors who foster a culture of meritocracy, adaptability, and expertise.

Ultimately, nepotism is a silent but destructive force that can erode the foundation of even the most successful organizations. While hiring or promoting trusted associates may seem like a safe and familiar choice, the long-term damage caused by favoritism far outweighs any short-term convenience. To build a strong, resilient organization, leaders must commit to hiring and promoting based on merit, ensuring that every role is filled by the most qualified individual—regardless of personal relationships.

Avoiding the Pitfall of Nepotism

The biggest issue I have with leadership is nepotism. Nepotism is the single most effective way to kill morale within an organization. When leaders hire friends, family members, or personal career cheerleaders, they send a clear message that loyalty and personal connections outweigh competence and hard work. This erodes trust, breeds resentment among employees, and ultimately weakens the firm's performance and reputation. Over time, nepotism fosters a toxic work environment where qualified employees feel overlooked, innovation stagnates, and the most capable team members either disengage or leave altogether.

To prevent nepotism from poisoning the workplace, leaders must enforce transparent hiring and promotion policies based strictly on merit, experience, and qualifications. Every decision should be guided by measurable criteria, ensuring that job postings are open to a diverse pool of candidates, interviews are standardized, and selections are made based on clearly defined qualifications rather than personal affiliations. A failure to do so not only undermines the organization's credibility but also creates an inner circle of favoritism that stifles growth and discourages true leadership development.

Objectivity in recruitment must be a non-negotiable standard, with structured evaluations, skills assessments, and verified references taking precedence over informal conversations or personal relationships. Leaders must recognize that every time they hire or promote based on connections rather than capability, they erode trust in leadership and foster an environment where mediocrity thrives. By prioritizing fairness and transparency, organizations can ensure that employees feel valued for their contributions rather than disillusioned by an unfair system, ultimately fostering a culture of excellence, trust, and long-term success.

The Importance of Clear Performance Metrics

One of the best ways to ensure fairness is by establishing clear, measurable performance metrics for both hiring and promotions. Every role within an organization should have defined Key Performance Indicators (KPIs) and success benchmarks so that employees know exactly what is expected to earn recognition and advancement. When performance evaluations are tied to data-driven assessments, it becomes easier to distinguish top performers from those who merely benefit from personal connections. However, fairness alone is not enough, accountability is equally critical.

Holding all leaders to the same level of accountability is essential for an organization to run smoothly and to foster a culture of trust and high performance. If leadership is exempt from the same expectations and standards applied to employees, it breeds resentment and discourages hard work. Leaders must set an example by demonstrating transparency in decision-making, adhering to established policies, and ensuring that no one, regardless of title or tenure, is above the rules.

By using quantifiable goals, peer reviews, and structured performance assessments, organizations eliminate ambiguity and favoritism from the decision-making process. When employees see that promotions are earned through results rather than relationships, they are more likely to remain engaged, motivated, and committed to company success. A culture of accountability ensures that every individual, from entry-level employees to executives, is held to the same high standards, reinforcing fairness and driving organizational excellence.

Creating a Culture of Fairness and Equal Opportunity

Avoiding nepotism is not just about policies and processes, it requires an organizational culture that values fairness, equal opportunity, and accountability at all levels. Leaders must set the tone by demonstrating integrity in their hiring practices and holding others accountable for upholding these standards.

One way to reinforce fairness is through diverse hiring panels and decision-making committees that prevent anyone from having undue influence over a hiring or promotion decision. When multiple perspectives are involved in evaluating candidates, it reduces the likelihood of favoritism creeping into the process.

Additionally, leaders must create avenues for employees to report favoritism or unethical hiring practices without fear of retaliation. Whether through anonymous feedback systems, HR oversight, or independent review boards, employees should feel confident that they are working in an organization that values talent and contribution over personal ties.

The Role of Leadership in Setting the Example

Leaders must lead by example in avoiding nepotism. This means not only refraining from hiring family, friends, and their cheerleaders but also resisting the urge to hire those who are simply agreeable or familiar. Too often, leaders select candidates based on personal comfort rather than professional capability. Instead, leaders should seek to build teams with the best possible talent, even if that means hiring individuals who challenge them, bring new ideas, or come from different backgrounds.

I have personally seen nepotism undermine organizations, which is why, when I ran my own company, I refused to hire family members, friends, or people simply because I liked them. More importantly, I never hired based on personal preference—I hired to win. This distinction is what separates successful organizations from those that stagnate. Winning organizations hire for skill, innovation, and expertise, not familiarity or personal loyalty. I have always run my companies with this personal motto:

"If you want to be the best, you must hire the best, avoid the rest"

Avoiding nepotism requires commitment, discipline, and a willingness to prioritize merit over comfort. Organizations that implement transparent hiring processes, objective performance metrics, and a culture of fairness will not only avoid the pitfalls of favoritism but will also attract the best talent, retain high performers, and build a reputation for excellence. In the end, leaders who hire based on competence rather than connections create organizations that thrive, innovate, and endure.

The Cost of Rushed Decisions

Hiring the right people is one of the most critical functions of leadership. The strength of an organization is directly tied to the quality of its workforce, and every hiring decision has long-term implications for performance, culture, and overall success. Yet, too many leaders rush the hiring process, fail to properly vet candidates, or prioritize short-term convenience over long-term fit. Whether due to urgency, pressure to fill a role, or a lack of structured hiring procedures, poor hiring practices can create significant disruptions that ripple across the entire organization. "Promote competence, not connections."

"Favoritism breeds failure; accountability drives success"

The consequences of hasty or ill-considered hiring decisions extend far beyond a single bad hire. Poor hiring choices lead to high turnover, drain organizational resources, lower morale, and disrupt team dynamics. A single misstep in hiring can set off a chain reaction of inefficiencies, forcing organizations to waste time and money on rehiring, retraining, and repairing the damage caused by a poorly chosen employee. When leaders fail to hire strategically, the costs are steep—not just in financial terms, but in lost productivity, diminished morale, and weakened company culture.

"Hire for talent, not ties—success depends on merit, not loyalty"

How Poor Hiring Practices Hurt Organizations

Hiring is one of the most critical decisions an organization makes, yet many leaders underestimate its long-term impact. A single poor hiring decision can set off a chain reaction of inefficiencies, low morale, and financial losses, affecting not just the new hire but the entire team. When organizations rush the hiring process, fail to properly vet candidates, or prioritize filling a vacancy over finding the right fit, they compromise performance, productivity, and workplace culture.

"A single bad hire can cost a company money; repeated bad hires can cost a company its culture"

Poor hiring practices don't just affect immediate operations, they weaken the foundation of an organization over time. From high turnover rates to misaligned skills and disengaged employees, the consequences of ineffective hiring can be costly and difficult to reverse. A strong team starts with strong hiring decisions, and when organizations fail in this area, the damage can be widespread and long-lasting.

"When leaders choose comfort over competence, they trade short-term ease for long-term failure"

Hiring the right person is one of the most critical responsibilities of any leader. Yet, far too often, organizations rush the hiring process, focusing more on filling a vacancy than ensuring they are bringing in the right talent. The consequences of these missteps go far beyond a single bad hire—poor hiring decisions ripple through an organization, leading to lost productivity, high turnover, and a demoralized workforce.

A strong team is the foundation of any successful business. When hiring is done correctly, new employees enhance collaboration, drive innovation, and contribute to a thriving work culture. But when hiring is rushed, poorly executed, or misaligned with company needs, the fallout can be disastrous. From mismatched skills and cultural clashes to costly turnover and declining morale, poor hiring practices undermine organizational stability and efficiency.

This section explores some of the most common and costly hiring mistakes companies make—and, more importantly, how leaders can avoid them. By understanding the impact of hiring missteps, organizations can build a recruitment strategy that not only attracts top talent but also retains and nurtures employees who truly align with the company's vision and values; here are some examples:

Mismatched Skills and Culture Fit

Another common pitfall of poor hiring practices is failing to assess whether a candidate has both the necessary skills and the right cultural fit for the organization. Skill mismatches occur when candidates lack the technical competencies required for the job, leading to underperformance, frustration, and inefficiencies. However, an equally damaging mistake is hiring someone who does not align with the organization's values, work ethic, or team culture.

Employees who do not fit the company culture can disrupt team cohesion, create internal conflicts, and lower overall engagement. A

32

high-performing team relies on collaboration, trust, and shared goals—introducing an employee who clashes with these dynamics throws off team synergy and creates unnecessary friction.

Leaders who fail to properly vet candidates often prioritize filling a vacancy quickly rather than ensuring the new hire will be an asset to the organization. But a bad hire is worse than no hire at all—while an unfilled position may cause temporary strain, hiring the wrong person leads to lasting damage that can be far harder to fix.

Costly Turnover

Hiring is one of the most expensive investments a company makes, with recruitment, onboarding, and training costs quickly adding up, only to skyrocket if a bad hire leads to turnover. Getting it right the first time isn't just about finding the right fit; it's about protecting the organization's resources, maintaining team morale, and ensuring long-term stability. Rushed hiring decisions often result in employees leaving within months, forcing the organization to restart the hiring process from scratch. High turnover is one of the most expensive consequences of poor hiring practices. The cost of turnover includes:

- Recruitment expenses (advertising, headhunters, interview processes)

- Training and onboarding costs for new hires

- Lost productivity as new employees take time to ramp up

- Disruptions to existing teams, who must compensate for the loss of staff

The hidden cost of turnover is even more damaging—when employees leave, they take institutional knowledge with them, leaving gaps that reduce efficiency and create setbacks in ongoing projects.

Turnover also affects a company's brand and reputation. If an organization gains a reputation for frequent employee churn, top-tier talent will avoid applying, making future hiring even more difficult.

Companies that consistently struggle with retention signal instability, poor management, or a toxic work environment—none of which attract high-performing candidates.

Morale and Productivity

Poor hiring practices don't just impact the individual being hired—they affect the entire team. A revolving door of employees creates an environment of instability, making it difficult for teams to build strong, cohesive working relationships.

When existing employees are constantly training new hires, dealing with underqualified team members, or picking up the slack for poor hiring decisions, their engagement and motivation suffer. Frustration builds as employees feel like they are carrying more than their fair share of the workload. Over time, this results in:

- Decreased job satisfaction

- Lower trust in leadership decision-making

- Higher risk of burnout and turnover

- Reduced collaboration and innovation

Employees want to work in an environment where they can grow, contribute meaningfully, and be surrounded by competent colleagues. When teams see that leadership repeatedly hires the wrong people, rushes hiring decisions, or ignores clear red flags, they lose confidence in leadership's ability to manage effectively. A lack of trust in hiring decisions leads to disengagement, which ultimately reduces performance across the organization.

Avoiding Poor Hiring Practices

Effective leaders understand that hiring the right people is an investment, not just a task to check off a list. Prioritizing quality hires over speed ensures that new hires align with both the demands of their role and the overall mission of the organization. A well-thought-out hiring process saves time, money, and frustration in the long run. To avoid the trap of poor hiring practices, organizations should implement the following strategies:

Establish a Rigorous Hiring Process

A structured hiring process helps eliminate bias, inconsistency, and subjective decision-making that often leads to bad hires. This should include:

- Clearly defined job descriptions that outline the necessary skills, experience, and cultural fit criteria

- Multiple rounds of interviews with standardized questions to assess technical and soft skills

- Behavioral assessments to evaluate problem-solving, communication, and adaptability

- Reference checks and background screening to validate claims and assess past performance

Leaders should resist the urge to "go with their gut"—decisions should be based on data, competency, and potential, not personal preferences or a candidate's likability.

Focus on Retention, Not Just Recruitment

Hiring is only the first step—keeping employees engaged, challenged, and motivated is just as important as bringing them in. Organizations must invest in employee retention strategies, including:

- Proper onboarding programs that integrate new hires into the company culture

- Ongoing mentorship and career development opportunities

- Performance reviews with clear, actionable feedback

- A supportive workplace culture where employees feel valued and heard

By creating an environment where employees want to stay and grow, organizations significantly reduce turnover and ensure that hiring efforts yield long-term benefits.

Wait for the Right Candidate

One of the biggest hiring mistakes leaders make is filling a position just to fill it, even when the right candidate has not been found. A vacant role is better than a bad hire. Rushing to hire the wrong person only leads to wasted time, resources, and morale damage when that hire inevitably fails.

Leaders must exercise patience and discipline in hiring, ensuring that every person brought into the organization is truly the best fit. A slow and deliberate hiring process results in fewer mistakes, lower turnover, and stronger teams.

Poor hiring practices are one of the most damaging yet avoidable pitfalls in leadership. The consequences—high turnover, low morale, wasted resources, and diminished productivity—can cripple an organization's ability to perform at its best.

Successful leaders hire for skill, culture fit, and long-term success rather than making impulsive, short-sighted decisions. By implementing rigorous hiring processes, prioritizing retention, and waiting for the right candidate rather than settling for convenience, organizations can build high performing, engaged, and loyal teams that drive sustainable success.

Ultimately, hiring is not just about filling a seat, it's about shaping the future of the organization. Leaders who recognize the importance of quality hiring and retention strategies position their companies for long-term stability, growth, and innovation.

The Leadership Trust Killer

Accountability is the foundation of strong leadership and one of the most critical factors in an organization's success or failure. When leaders fail to take responsibility for their actions, they create a toxic culture of blame, disengagement, and stagnation that spreads throughout the organization. Employees look to leadership for guidance, fairness, and consistency, and when accountability is lacking at the top, it sends a clear signal that deflection, excuses, and complacency are acceptable. This failure in leadership does not go unnoticed—it erodes trust, decreases motivation, and ultimately weakens overall performance.

A leader who avoids responsibility sets a dangerous precedent, fostering an environment where problems are ignored rather than addressed, mistakes are covered up rather than learned from, and mediocrity is tolerated rather than challenged. Employees in such organizations quickly lose confidence in leadership, disengage from their work, and stop taking ownership of their responsibilities. Without accountability, teams become fragmented, communication breaks down, and decision-making is riddled with inefficiencies. What starts as a minor leadership failure can quickly snowball into widespread dysfunction, where employees no longer feel invested in their roles and innovation grinds to a halt.

Without accountability, organizations experience a breakdown in team cohesion, loss of credibility, and ultimately, high attrition rates. Talented employees, those who value integrity and professional growth, are often the first to leave, unwilling to work in an environment where leadership refuses to take ownership of failures or missteps. Those who remain may adopt the same lack of accountability, shifting blame and avoiding difficult conversations rather than working toward solutions. As this culture takes hold, poor performance becomes the norm, and the organization enters a cycle of stagnation, inefficiency, and continuous underperformance.

Conversely, organizations that prioritize accountability foster a culture of trust, ownership, and continuous improvement. Employees want to work in a place where leadership owns its decisions, acknowledges mistakes, and takes proactive steps to improve. A workplace that embraces accountability empowers employees to take initiative, solve problems, and feel a sense of pride in their contributions. Leaders who set the right example by holding themselves to high standards and demanding the same from their teams create environments where honesty, integrity, and responsibility drive both individual and organizational success.

"Say what you'll do and do what you say." -W. Edwards Deming

How Lack of Accountability Destroys Organizations

A workplace without accountability quickly turns into a breeding ground for finger-pointing, deflection, and excuse-making. When leaders refuse to take responsibility, employees follow their example, shifting blame rather than seeking solutions. Instead of learning from mistakes and improving processes, employees become preoccupied with avoiding fault, covering up errors, or placing responsibility on others. This culture of blame leads to a toxic work environment, where employees fear repercussions rather than feel empowered to take initiative. Mistakes are not addressed, inefficiencies go unchecked, and innovation is stifled. In contrast, organizations with high accountability foster a mindset of problem-solving, where failures are seen as opportunities for growth rather than excuses for punishment.

Trust is the foundation of any successful organization, and nothing destroys trust faster than a lack of accountability at the leadership level. Employees respect leaders who admit when they are wrong, take corrective action, and hold themselves to the same standards as everyone else. However, when leaders consistently shift blame, refuse to acknowledge issues, or ignore concerns, they lose credibility. Employees begin to feel disconnected, undervalued, and unmotivated. Over time, disengagement sets in, leading to lower productivity, increased absenteeism, and ultimately, high turnover rates. Employees who do not trust their leadership are far more likely to seek opportunities elsewhere, taking their skills, experience, and institutional knowledge with them. A revolving door of talent is one of the clearest indicators of a leadership failure rooted in a lack of accountability.

When accountability is absent, there is no incentive to improve, no urgency to fix problems, and no culture of continuous growth. Teams become complacent, resistant to feedback, and ultimately ineffective in achieving organizational goals. Without strong leadership to drive accountability, performance plateaus or declines, and mediocrity becomes the norm rather than the exception. Organizations that fail to hold leaders and employees accountable often find themselves repeating the same mistakes, struggling to adapt, and falling behind competitors. In contrast, high-accountability organizations encourage learning, innovation, and progress. Employees in these workplaces feel a sense of ownership and pride in their work, which fuels creativity, efficiency, and long-term success.

Avoiding the Pitfall of Lack of Accountability

The most effective leaders lead by example, taking ownership of both their successes and failures. They demonstrate integrity and set a standard for the entire organization by holding themselves accountable first. This fosters a culture where employees feel empowered to take responsibility for their work, learn from mistakes, and continuously strive for improvement. When accountability is ingrained in an organization's culture, employees are more engaged, motivated, and willing to take initiative.

To cultivate accountability, organizations must establish clear performance metrics that define measurable goals and expectations for employees at all levels. When everyone knows what success looks like, accountability becomes an inherent part of the culture. Regular feedback loops—including frequent performance evaluations, one-on-one meetings, and open communication channels—help ensure that accountability is consistently reinforced. Leaders should not only provide constructive feedback but also be open to receiving it, demonstrating that accountability applies to everyone.

Creating transparent evaluation processes is essential to fostering a fair and accountable workplace. Promotions, raises, and disciplinary actions should be based on objective performance data rather than favoritism or office politics. Employees are more likely to hold themselves accountable when they see that leadership recognizes and rewards accountability fairly. Additionally, organizations should encourage a mindset of learning rather than punishment. By reframing mistakes as opportunities for growth rather than failures, employees will feel more comfortable acknowledging missteps, improving their performance, and contributing to a culture of continuous development. When accountability is embraced at all levels, organizations become stronger, more efficient, and more resilient in the face of challenges.

Accountability is not optional, it is essential to building trust, driving engagement, and ensuring long-term success. Leaders who fail to take responsibility create environments where blame replaces problem-solving, trust deteriorates, and stagnation sets in. Without accountability, organizations lose credibility, struggle with high turnover, and fail to inspire employees to perform at their best.

The most successful organizations are those where accountability is embraced at every level, from the leadership team to frontline employees. Leaders who own their decisions, good or bad, admit mistakes, and continuously strive for improvement set the foundation for a thriving, innovative, and resilient workplace. In the end, accountability is the difference between a failing organization and one that grows, adapts, and leads.

Silent Killer of Progress is Resistance to Change

The world is constantly evolving, and organizations must adapt to stay competitive. Yet, many leaders resist change out of fear, complacency, or arrogance. Whether due to comfort in familiar processes, skepticism about new approaches, or reluctance to disrupt the status quo, leaders who fail to innovate, embrace new technologies, or adapt to shifting market demands risk irrelevance and organizational decline. The inability to evolve with industry trends, customer expectations, or technological advancements places organizations at a severe disadvantage, making them vulnerable to more agile competitors.

Resistance to change hinders innovation and growth by stifling new ideas before they can take root. Leaders who refuse to adapt prevent their organizations from progressing, ultimately stalling advancement and limiting long-term success. A rigid leadership approach can also result in the loss of competitive advantage. Industries evolve rapidly, and companies that fail to keep pace are inevitably left behind. Blockbuster's failure to embrace streaming technology is a prime example of how resisting change can lead to obsolescence. While Netflix and other streaming services capitalized on changing consumer behaviors, Blockbuster remained fixated on its outdated rental model, ultimately leading to its downfall.

Beyond business performance, a fear-based culture often emerges in organizations resistant to change. Employees in such workplaces become hesitant to challenge the status quo, share new ideas, or take risks, fearing that leadership will reject or dismiss their contributions. When innovation is discouraged, stagnation takes hold, and organizations miss out on valuable opportunities for growth and improvement. In contrast, organizations that foster adaptability create environments where employees feel empowered to contribute ideas, experiment with new strategies, and drive progress.

Successful leaders view change as an opportunity rather than a threat. They cultivate a culture of innovation by encouraging experimentation, rewarding adaptability, and proactively staying ahead of industry trends. By maintaining an open-minded approach and actively engaging employees in the change process, leaders ensure that transitions are smoother, resistance is minimized, and the organization remains resilient in a constantly shifting business landscape. Organizations that embrace change rather than resist it position themselves for long-term success, continuous improvement, and sustained growth.

Finally, leadership failure is not inevitable, but it is often the result of avoidable mistakes. Nepotism, poor hiring practices, lack of accountability, and resistance to change are all pitfalls that undermine trust, efficiency, and long-term success. By recognizing these issues and actively working to correct them, leaders can foster a culture of fairness, responsibility, and innovation.

The most successful leaders are those who embrace accountability, prioritize competence over personal connections, hire strategically, and remain adaptable in the face of change. Avoiding these common pitfalls is not just about preventing failure, it is about building a thriving, resilient organization that can withstand the test of time.

"Nepotism, poor hiring, lack of accountability, and resistance to change are the silent architects of failure—eroding trust, crippling efficiency, and sabotaging long-term success"

Chapter 3

Building Strong Leadership Teams

Astrong leadership team is the backbone of any successful organization. Great leaders inspire, guide, and set the standard for performance and culture. However, building an effective leadership team requires intentional effort, structured processes, and a commitment to continuous improvement. Without a solid foundation of capable leaders, an organization will be in a constant state of faltering, stumbling from one failure to the next, bogged down by the missteps of would-be leaders whose primary concern isn't the organization's mission or goals, but rather their own career advancement. These individuals are often yes-men and yes-women, more focused on appeasing higher-ups and protecting their positions than on making tough, necessary decisions that drive real progress.

"Great leadership teams aren't built by hiring stars; they're built by aligning strengths and fostering trust"

In this chapter, we will explore key strategies for cultivating strong leadership teams, from establishing a merit-based culture and improving hiring processes to fostering accountability and embracing innovation. Additionally, we will examine the pitfalls of leadership by classroom, where individuals mistake theoretical knowledge for real-world leadership capability. By analyzing both leadership failures and successes, we will identify the traits and strategies that separate mediocre leaders from exceptional ones. A thriving organization isn't built on self-serving opportunities, it is built on a leadership team that knows how to execute, adapt, and inspire at every level.

Establishing a Merit-Based Culture

One of the fundamental pillars of a strong leadership team is a culture rooted in meritocracy. When leadership roles are assigned based on competence, performance, and potential rather than favoritism or tenure, organizations thrive. A merit-based culture ensures that the best individuals rise to leadership positions, driving innovation, engagement, and efficiency.

> *"A strong leadership team isn't a collection of titles, it's a coalition of purpose, vision, and accountability"*

To achieve this, organizations must implement transparent performance evaluations and reward systems. Leadership assessments should be data-driven, measurable, and regularly reviewed to ensure that promotions and leadership decisions are based on performance rather than politics. Rewarding strong leadership not only incentivizes excellence but also signals to employees that leadership roles are earned, not handed out based on connections.

Professional development is another crucial aspect of a merit-based culture. Organizations that prioritize leadership training, mentorship programs, and career progression opportunities retain top talent and cultivate a leadership pipeline of individuals prepared to take on greater responsibilities. Encouraging continuous learning, skill development, and adaptability ensures that the leadership team remains effective, forward-thinking, and prepared for evolving challenges.

Enhancing Hiring Processes

The foundation of a strong leadership team starts with hiring the right people. A bad hiring decision can have lasting consequences, impacting morale, productivity, and long-term growth. Organizations that refine and strengthen their hiring processes are far more likely to cultivate effective leaders who align with company values and goals.

A well-structured hiring process begins with clear, well-defined job descriptions. Leadership roles must have specific expectations, required competencies, and clear measures of success. Ambiguity in job descriptions invites misalignment between leadership expectations and performance.

"The best leadership teams are like orchestras—each member plays a unique part, but together, they create harmony"

Once a strong candidate pool is established, structured interviews should be used to assess leadership potential. A consistent, standardized interview process ensures that all candidates are evaluated fairly and objectively. Instead of relying on gut feelings or personal biases, leaders should use behavioral assessments and reference checks to gauge a candidate's ability to manage teams, handle conflict, and drive results. These extra layers of evaluation help organizations make informed hiring decisions and prevent the costly mistake of placing the wrong person in a leadership role.

Promoting Accountability

Accountability is the glue that holds a leadership team together. Without it, even the most talented leaders will fail to meet objectives, build trust, or drive progress. Organizations must establish clear expectations, measurable goals, and regular progress reviews to ensure that leaders are held responsible for their performance and decisions.

A key strategy for promoting accountability is setting measurable goals and defining key performance indicators (KPIs) for leadership roles. Leaders should not just be evaluated based on financial outcomes but also on team engagement, decision-making effectiveness, and problem-solving skills. Regular performance reviews and leadership evaluations provide opportunities for self-reflection, course correction, and continuous improvement.

"Building a great leadership team means valuing the dissenting voice, because innovation thrives on perspective"

Beyond metrics, creating a feedback culture is critical to sustaining accountability. In strong leadership teams, both successes and failures are openly discussed. When mistakes occur, leaders should own them, learn from them, and apply those lessons moving forward. Encouraging honest conversations about areas for improvement strengthens trust, fosters resilience, and prevents a culture of blame or secrecy.

Embracing Change and Innovation

Strong leadership teams thrive on adaptability. In a world where industries, technologies, and customer expectations evolve rapidly, leaders who resist change risk leading their organizations into stagnation and decline. The most effective leadership teams embrace change as an opportunity rather than a threat, fostering a culture of experimentation, learning, and forward-thinking strategies.

One of the best ways to foster innovation is to reward adaptability and calculated risk-taking. Leaders who are encouraged to experiment with new ideas, fail fast, and iterate on improvements contribute to an environment where creativity flourishes. In contrast, organizations that punish failure discourage bold thinking, leading to stagnation and missed opportunities.

"The foundation of a great leadership team isn't agreement—it's respect, collaboration, and a shared commitment to success"

Additionally, data-driven decision-making should be a core leadership practice. Leaders who rely on intuition alone often make costly mistakes, while those who incorporate market trends, employee insights, and performance analytics make informed, strategic choices. By staying ahead of industry trends and continuously challenging outdated assumptions, leadership teams position their organizations for long-term success and resilience.

Leadership by Classroom?

One of the most damaging misconceptions about leadership is the belief that a leadership degree, seminar, or certificate alone qualifies someone to lead. This type of leadership is just The Illusion of Leadership Expertise and can create resentment. Many individuals fall into the trap of assuming that because they took a leadership class, attended a seminar, or earned a low-quality leadership degree, they are now authorities on leadership. However, leadership is not something that can be taught in a classroom, it must be learned through experience, tested under pressure, and refined over time. Leadership is not just theoretical; it is practical, adaptive, and deeply tied to a person's innate traits, emotional intelligence, and ability to inspire and guide others.

> *"Leadership teams succeed not by avoiding challenges, but by facing them together with clarity and conviction"*

Courses, books, and degrees can teach leadership concepts, frameworks, and strategies, but they cannot instill true leadership ability in someone who lacks the fundamental qualities required to lead. If an individual does not naturally possess the ability to inspire, make tough decisions, and take responsibility, no amount of coursework will turn them into an effective leader. At best, they will learn how to manage processes, follow leadership theories, and check administrative boxes, but they will never develop the instinctive ability to rally a team, take decisive action under uncertainty, or navigate the complexities of human dynamics that true leadership demands.

This is where many self-proclaimed leaders fail. Some believe that simply telling others how to lead makes them effective leaders. These are the same people who memorize leadership principles and theories but struggle to apply them in real-world scenarios. They can quote leadership models, reference case studies, and discuss strategic frameworks, but when placed in a real leadership position, they falter, hesitate, or avoid the hard decisions that separate true leaders from those who merely hold a title. Leadership is not about understanding the concept of decision-making, but it is about having the confidence and instinct to make the right decision in critical moments.

The reality is that leadership and management are two entirely different things, and one does not automatically translate into the other. A person can be a great manager—capable of organizing tasks, enforcing policies, and ensuring operational efficiency—without being a leader. A manager directs people, but a leader inspires them. Managers ensure that processes run smoothly, deadlines are met, and productivity remains consistent, but leaders create vision, drive innovation, and inspire people to achieve more than they thought possible.

"A team of leaders isn't defined by individual brilliance but by collective resilience and the ability to inspire action in others"

Conversely, someone can be a phenomenal leader but a poor manager. They might have an extraordinary ability to inspire, motivate, and make bold decisions but struggle with administrative duties, process enforcement, or logistics. True leadership is about guiding people, making decisions under uncertainty, and having the emotional intelligence to navigate complex interpersonal dynamics. Management is about execution, structure, and ensuring day-to-day tasks are completed efficiently. The two skill sets do not always align, and many organizations make the mistake of assuming that a good manager will automatically make a good leader—or that a person with a leadership degree is fit to lead.

However, in rare cases, you find that one person in a hundred who possesses both exceptional leadership and strong managerial capabilities. These individuals can both inspire and execute, both lead with vision and manage with precision. They are the ones who can see the bigger picture while also ensuring that every small detail is accounted for. These dual-skilled individuals are extraordinarily rare, but when found, they become invaluable assets to any organization.

True leadership is not something that can be taught in a classroom, nor is it something that can be acquired simply by earning a degree. It is earned through experience, self-awareness, and the ability to navigate challenges in the real world. Leaders who lack real-world experience often make misguided decisions, fail to connect with their teams, and struggle to inspire confidence. The best leaders blend knowledge with action, continuously refining their approach based on lived experiences rather than academic exercises. Great leaders are not created by textbooks; they are forged in the fires of real-world challenges, adversity, and responsibility.

Case Studies of Leadership Failures

History is filled with examples of leadership failures caused by poor hiring decisions, lack of accountability, resistance to change, and overconfidence in theoretical knowledge. Many organizations that once thrived ultimately collapsed because their leadership failed to adapt, made unethical choices, or prioritized short-term gains over long-term sustainability. Companies that resisted innovation allowed nepotism to dictate leadership roles or failed to foster transparency in decision-making found themselves unable to keep up with industry shifts, leading to irreversible consequences. These failures serve as stark warnings for future leaders on what not to do when building leadership teams.

"A great leadership team doesn't compete for the spotlight, it builds the stage for others to shine"

One of the most infamous leadership failures is Enron's collapse, which stemmed from a culture of greed, unethical decision-making, and a complete lack of accountability at the executive level. Enron executives manipulated financial statements, engaged in fraudulent accounting practices, and prioritized short-term stock gains over ethical business operations. Leadership fostered an environment of secrecy and arrogance, silencing whistleblowers and misleading investors until the company eventually imploded in one of the largest corporate bankruptcies in history. The Enron scandal highlights how a lack of integrity, transparency, and ethical leadership can destroy even the most promising companies.

Another well-known failure is Blockbuster's downfall, a prime example of what happens when leaders resist change and ignore market shifts. Blockbuster once dominated the video rental industry but failed to anticipate the rise of digital streaming and online entertainment. Leadership dismissed multiple opportunities to innovate, including passing on the chance to acquire Netflix for a fraction of its current value. Instead of adapting to shifting consumer behavior, Blockbuster's executives remained fixated on their outdated rental model. By the time they attempted to launch their own streaming service, Netflix had already established dominance, and Blockbuster's decline was inevitable. This case demonstrates the dangers of complacency in leadership and the importance of staying ahead of industry trends.

"Diversity in thought and unity in purpose—that's the DNA of a transformative leadership team"

Beyond the corporate world, political and military failures also highlight the consequences of poor leadership. The handling of Hurricane Katrina in 2005 by federal, state, and local officials is a striking example of how a lack of preparedness, miscommunication, and failure to take responsibility can turn a crisis into a catastrophe. Delayed responses, lack of coordination, and leaders ignoring early warnings led to unnecessary loss of life and immense suffering. This case underscores the need for leaders to be decisive, accountable, and proactive in crisis situations.

"True leadership teams aren't built on authority; they're built on shared purpose and mutual respect"

Each of these failures offers valuable lessons about leadership. Ignoring innovation, resisting change, failing to uphold ethical standards, and neglecting accountability are sure paths to organizational disaster. Strong leadership isn't about maintaining the status quo, it's about adapting, making hard decisions, and always acting with integrity.

Case Studies of Leadership Success

In contrast, successful organizations demonstrate the power of strong leadership teams that embrace change, foster accountability, and drive innovation. Companies that prioritize long-term vision, invest in leadership development, and create a culture of adaptability consistently outperform their competitors. Some of the most successful companies and institutions in history have thrived because of leaders who were willing to challenge norms, take calculated risks, and surround themselves with the right people.

First, Amazon is a perfect example of a company that succeeded due to visionary leadership and continuous innovation. Jeff Bezos built Amazon into a global powerhouse by embracing change, anticipating market trends, and taking bold risks. Unlike Blockbuster, which clung to its outdated model, Amazon continuously evolved—from an online bookstore to a leader in e-commerce, cloud computing, and artificial intelligence. Bezos prioritized customer experience, efficiency, and long-term growth over short-term profits, allowing Amazon to dominate multiple industries. His leadership strategy demonstrates the importance of adaptability, long-term vision, and customer-centric decision-making.

Second, Tesla under Elon Musk, a company that revolutionized the automotive industry through disruptive innovation and bold decision-making. Musk's leadership style, though unconventional, has pushed Tesla to the forefront of electric vehicle technology and sustainable energy. His ability to take risks, challenge traditional automotive norms, and prioritize technological advancements has not only made Tesla a market leader but has also forced the entire auto industry to adapt. Tesla's success highlights the importance of a strong vision, persistence, and willingness to challenge the status quo.

Beyond the corporate world, military and political history provides numerous examples of exceptional leadership. Winston Churchill's leadership during World War II is a classic example of strong, decisive leadership in times of crisis. Churchill's ability to inspire confidence, make tough decisions, and rally a nation during one of its darkest periods showcases the power of effective leadership under immense pressure. His ability to communicate vision and resilience in the face of adversity was instrumental in maintaining morale and strategic focus.

These success stories highlight the critical role that strong leadership strategies play in shaping the long-term growth and sustainability of any organization. The best leaders surround themselves with talented individuals, encourage innovation, hold themselves accountable, and take calculated risks. They recognize that leadership isn't about maintaining control, it's about guiding, inspiring, and ensuring the organization is always evolving and improving.

A Reality Check for Every Leader

Leadership isn't about titles, degrees, or charisma—it's about competence, accountability, and adaptability. It's about stepping up when others hesitate, making tough decisions when the easy path is to avoid them, and taking ownership when things go wrong instead of shifting blame. Organizations that prioritize merit over favoritism, refine their hiring practices to bring in true leaders rather than career cheerleaders, promote accountability at every level, and embrace change instead of fearing it are the ones that thrive. They don't just survive challenges; they innovate, inspire, and shape the future.

But what about the organizations that do the opposite? Those that reward incompetence, resist change, and rely on theoretical leadership over real-world execution? They don't just stagnate; they decline, erode trust, and ultimately collapse under the weight of their own dysfunction. Look around—how many companies, institutions, and even governments have suffered because of leadership failures? How many times have you seen unqualified individuals rise to power, not because they were the best, but because they played the game better?

Now, turn the lens inward. What kind of leader are you? Are you someone who inspires, makes tough calls, and takes responsibility, or do you avoid conflict, make excuses, and let outdated methods guide your decisions? Do you build others up, or do you hold onto authority because it makes you feel powerful? Are you willing to adapt, evolve, and challenge yourself to be a better leader every day?

Great leadership teams don't just happen—they are built with intention, discipline, and an unwavering commitment to continuous learning. If you want to lead effectively, you must demand excellence from yourself first. By implementing the strategies in this chapter, organizations—and individuals—can cultivate leadership that doesn't just occupy positions of power, but actively drives innovation, sustains competitive advantages, and leads with integrity and purpose. The question is: Are you ready to be that kind of leader?

"Leadership isn't about being in charge—it's about building others up, so together you achieve what no one could alone"

Chapter 4

Lessons from Failed Leadership

Leadership is often romanticized as a pathway to success, but history has repeatedly shown that poor leadership can be just as impactful, only in the wrong direction. Organizations rise and fall on the backs of their leaders, and when those in power fail to lead effectively, the consequences ripple through entire teams, industries, and even economies. Leadership failure isn't always the result of a single catastrophic mistake, it's usually a combination of poor judgment, resistance to change, lack of vision, and an inability to inspire and empower others.

In this chapter, we will examine the most common leadership failures that derail organizations, explore real-world case studies of leadership gone wrong, and extract valuable lessons that leaders at all levels can apply to avoid these pitfalls.

Failure to Communicate Vision and Goals

A leader without a clear vision and the ability to communicate it is like a captain sailing without a map—directionless, lost, and doomed to fail. Vision is what gives an organization purpose, direction, and momentum. It's what aligns teams, drives strategic decisions, and fosters a sense of shared mission. Without it, an organization wanders aimlessly, reacting to challenges instead of proactively shaping its future. One of the most common and damaging leadership failures is the inability to articulate a clear and compelling vision for their team or organization.

Clarity is the foundation of execution. Leaders who fail to define and communicate specific goals, expectations, and purpose leave employees confused and disengaged. When people don't understand the bigger picture or their role within it, they become demotivated, uncertain, and hesitant in their work. Tasks become fragmented, decision-making becomes inconsistent, and employees end up operating in silos, often working against each other rather than toward a unified goal. Misalignment leads to inefficiencies, frustration, and wasted effort, as employees struggle to determine what is truly important.

Some leaders make the critical mistake of assuming that employees "just understand" what needs to be done. They believe that their vision is obvious, expecting their teams to figure out objectives without explicit direction. This assumption creates an environment of inefficiency and frustration, where employees second-guess themselves, duplicate efforts, or prioritize the wrong tasks. Without a well-communicated vision, resources are misallocated, strategic decision-making becomes reactive rather than proactive, and morale declines as employees feel like they are working without purpose or recognition.

The long-term effects of poor vision communication are severe. Over time, confusion turns into disengagement, disengagement turns into turnover, and turnover weakens the organization as a whole. Internal conflict arises as different departments or teams pull in different directions, unsure of how their efforts contribute to the overall strategy. The result? A lack of momentum, stagnation, and ultimately, failure to achieve long-term success.

Successful leaders understand that communication is not just about speaking, it's about ensuring understanding. They don't just announce their vision once and assume everyone gets it; they embed it into everyday conversations, reinforce it through strategic initiatives, and connect it to individual roles within the organization. They reiterate goals regularly, clarify expectations, and ensure that every team member understands how their work contributes to the broader mission. When a leader communicates vision effectively, they don't just tell people what to do, they inspire them to believe in the mission, take ownership of their role, and work together to make that vision a reality.

Trust is the Cornerstone of Leadership

Trust is the foundation of all effective leadership; without it, a leader is nothing more than a figurehead. Employees need to believe that their leader has their best interests at heart, will make fair and ethical decisions, and will follow through on their commitments. When trust is strong, it creates a culture of collaboration, loyalty, and high performance. But when trust is broken, it can be nearly impossible to repair, leading to disengagement, dysfunction, and ultimately, failure.

A leader's credibility and influence are entirely dependent on the trust they cultivate. Leaders who are perceived as dishonest, inconsistent, or self-serving quickly lose the respect and commitment of their teams. Employees who don't trust their leader will hold back their efforts, second-guess decisions, and eventually seek opportunities elsewhere. Even the most skilled employees will not give their full potential in an environment where they feel manipulated, ignored, or deceived. They begin to disengage, not because they lack ability, but because they lack faith in leadership.

Trust is fragile and can be broken in many ways. Empty promises, lack of follow-through, favoritism, or unethical behavior are among the most common trust killers. Leaders who say one thing but do another erode their credibility over time, leaving employees skeptical and resentful. Favoritism, where certain employees are granted special privileges or opportunities based on personal relationships rather than merit, creates division and resentment within teams. Ethical breaches, whether small lapses in honesty or major corporate scandals, destroy trust almost instantly and can permanently damage an organization's reputation.

A broken trust cycle leads to high turnover rates and a toxic workplace culture, where employees operate out of fear, skepticism, and self-preservation rather than engagement and collaboration. When employees don't trust their leaders, they stop offering ideas, taking initiative, and going above and beyond—because they don't believe their contributions will be recognized or valued. Over time, this creates a stagnant and disengaged workforce, where people show up only to collect a paycheck, not to drive results or innovation.

The best leaders earn and maintain trust by demonstrating transparency, consistency, and fairness. They own their mistakes, communicate openly, and follow through on commitments. Great leaders make decisions not based on personal ambition or short-term convenience, but on the best interests of their team and the organization as a whole. They recognize that trust is built in small moments but can be destroyed in an instant, so they act with integrity, honesty, and accountability in everything they do.

A leader who loses trust loses everything. But a leader who earns and protects trust will create a thriving, motivated, and high-performing team that stands by them in the face of challenges. The question every leader must ask themselves is: Are my actions building trust, or breaking it?

Failure to Decide or Making a Poor Decision

Decision-making is one of the most defining traits of a leader. Every choice, whether large or small, shapes the direction of an organization, influences team morale, and determines long-term success or failure. Yet, ineffective leaders often make impulsive, uninformed, or self-serving choices, leading to instability, financial losses, and declining trust among employees and stakeholders. Some leaders fail to make decisions at all, allowing problems to fester until they escalate into crises. Others make rash, emotion-driven decisions without considering the data, long-term consequences, or expert insights, resulting in poorly executed strategies and internal chaos.

The root cause of poor decision-making often lies in one or more of the following leadership failures:

- Ignoring Data and Analytics: Many leaders rely on gut instinct rather than hard evidence, choosing to make decisions based on past experiences, personal biases, or outdated assumptions. In today's data-driven world, failing to leverage available insights can lead to serious miscalculations. A leader who ignores financial reports, customer feedback, or market trends is essentially flying blind, making choices without a clear understanding of the landscape.

- Failure to Consult Stakeholders: Some leaders operate in isolation, believing they alone have the answers. They fail to seek input from experts, frontline employees, or key stakeholders, leading to decisions that are misaligned with reality. A leader who dismisses the insights of those closest to a problem—employees, customers, or advisors—risks making choices that are impractical, damaging, or out of touch with operational needs.

- Prioritizing Short-Term Gains Over Long-Term Success: Many poor decisions stem from a desire for immediate results rather than sustainable growth. Leaders who prioritize short-term cost-cutting over long-term investment, quick wins over lasting impact, or superficial fixes over strategic planning often leave their organizations vulnerable to long-term failure. This approach is particularly dangerous in business, politics, and crisis management, where short-sighted thinking can lead to catastrophic consequences.

- Letting Emotions Dictate Decisions: Emotion-driven decision-making can be as dangerous as indecision itself. Leaders who react impulsively to pressure, make choices based on personal conflicts, or let fear, anger, or ego drive their actions create inconsistent policies, chaotic work environments, and a lack of direction. A single emotionally charged decision—whether out of frustration, desperation, or pride—can have ripple effects that damage relationships, credibility, and organizational stability.

The consequences of poor decision-making can be devastating. A single bad call can result in financial losses, missed opportunities, loss of trust, and long-term damage to an organization's reputation. Poorly planned decisions often require costly reversals, undermining leadership credibility. Employees and stakeholders lose faith in a leader who frequently changes direction, enacts policies without explanation, or makes choices that contradict previous commitments.

On the other hand, great leaders understand that decision-making is a process, not a gamble. They take a methodical approach, ensuring that every major decision is backed by evidence, strategic thinking, and input from the right people. Effective leaders:

- Analyze Information Thoroughly: They collect and assess relevant data before making a move.

- Seek Input from Experts: They surround themselves with knowledgeable advisors and listen to diverse perspectives.

- Weigh Risks Carefully: They consider both short-term consequences and long-term impact.

- Remain Adaptable: They recognize that not every decision will be perfect, and they remain willing to course-correct when necessary.

Leadership is not about always making the right decision, it's about making the best decision possible with the available information, learning from mistakes, and having the humility to adjust when needed. The difference between successful and failed leadership often comes down to one simple factor: The ability to make sound, well-informed decisions.

Hidden Leadership Weakness

Leadership is not just about making strategic decisions or driving business results, it's about managing people, motivating teams, and creating an environment where individuals feel valued, heard, and empowered. At the heart of great leadership lies emotional intelligence (EQ), the ability to understand, manage, and navigate emotions in oneself and others. Leaders who lack emotional intelligence struggle to build strong relationships, resolve conflicts effectively, and inspire loyalty. Instead of fostering a cohesive and motivated workforce, they often alienate employees, create toxic environments, and unknowingly drive top talent away.

Leaders who lack self-awareness, empathy, and interpersonal skills frequently misread team dynamics, dismiss employee concerns, and fail to address conflicts before they escalate. This disconnect between leadership and employees results in low morale, frequent misunderstandings, and high turnover rates. Without emotional intelligence, a leader may inadvertently cause friction within teams, fail to recognize the emotional needs of their workforce, or struggle to communicate in a way that fosters trust and respect.

A lack of emotional intelligence can manifest in several damaging ways, including:

- Inability to Recognize Employee Frustration or Disengagement: A leader without EQ fails to see when employees are unhappy, overwhelmed, or feeling undervalued. Instead of recognizing warning signs such as disengagement, declining productivity, or increased absenteeism, they assume that employees are simply underperforming or not committed. This can lead to further frustration as employees feel unheard and unsupported.

- Poor Conflict Resolution Skills: Conflict is inevitable in any workplace, but leaders who lack emotional intelligence handle it poorly—often by avoiding difficult conversations, taking sides unfairly, or responding with emotional outbursts. Instead of facilitating productive discussions and finding resolutions, they allow tensions to fester, leading to distrust and divisions within the team.

- Difficulty Building Meaningful Connections: Employees want to feel valued and understood, yet leaders without emotional intelligence fail to establish real connections with their teams. They may appear distant, unapproachable, or overly transactional, making it difficult for employees to seek guidance, voice concerns, or feel a sense of belonging within the organization.

- Inconsistent or Emotionally Charged Leadership Style: Leaders without emotional intelligence react impulsively to stress, criticism, or challenges, often making rash decisions based on emotion rather than logic. Some may exhibit mood swings, where they are approachable one day and dismissive the next, leaving employees walking on eggshells, unsure of how their leader will respond in different situations.

On the other hand, successful leaders understand that people are the backbone of any organization. They prioritize relationships, listen actively, and foster an environment where employees feel valued and supported. These leaders recognize that their words, tone, and actions have a direct impact on team morale, motivation, and overall productivity.

Strong emotional intelligence enables leaders to:

- Recognize and manage their own emotions, ensuring that stress or frustration does not negatively affect their leadership style.

- Practice empathy, taking the time to understand different perspectives and acknowledge employee challenges.

- Communicate effectively, using active listening, clarity, and thoughtful responses to strengthen relationships and build trust.

- Encourage open dialogue, creating a safe space where employees feel heard and respected.

- Lead with consistency and fairness, making employees feel secure in their roles and confident in leadership decisions.

Emotional intelligence is not just a "nice-to-have" skill, it is essential for effective leadership. A leader with high EQ creates a workplace where employees are engaged, motivated, and willing to go the extra mile. Meanwhile, a leader who lacks emotional intelligence creates an environment of stress, uncertainty, and disengagement. The difference between a thriving team and one that struggles often comes down to how well a leader understands and manages emotions, both their own and those of their employees.

The Leadership Bottleneck

Some leaders mistakenly believe that control equals effectiveness, leading them to micromanage rather than trust their teams. They operate under the illusion that if they are involved in every detail, nothing can go wrong. However, micromanagement is one of the most damaging leadership failures—it stifles creativity, slows down processes, and demoralizes employees by fostering an environment of dependency rather than autonomy. Instead of empowering employees to take ownership of their work, micromanagers create a culture where people feel restricted, undervalued, and afraid to make decisions without approval.

Micromanagement often stems from a leader's insecurity, perfectionism, or fear of losing control. Some leaders believe that their way is the only right way, leading them to hover over employees, second-guess their decisions, and intervene unnecessarily. Others fear that delegating tasks will make them appear weak or replaceable, causing them to cling to responsibilities that should be shared. While their intentions may be to ensure quality and efficiency, the result is often the opposite—slower workflows, reduced innovation, and a workforce that feels frustrated and disengaged.

The Consequences of Micromanagement

Micromanagement is more than just an annoying habit—it has serious consequences for both employees and the organization as a whole:

- Reduced Creativity and Innovation: Employees need space to think, experiment, and contribute ideas. When a leader over-controls every decision, employees stop thinking creatively and simply follow instructions. This leads to a culture of compliance rather than innovation, where employees become passive rather than proactive problem solvers.

- Slower Decision-Making and Productivity: Micromanagers often insist on reviewing every detail, approving every step, and controlling every aspect of execution. This creates unnecessary bottlenecks, delaying projects and frustrating teams who feel they can't move forward without leadership intervention. Instead of streamlining operations, micromanagers add layers of inefficiency that slow progress and increase frustration.

- Low Employee Morale and Engagement: When employees feel distrusted or constantly scrutinized, their motivation declines. They begin to doubt their own abilities, hesitate to take initiative, and ultimately feel disengaged from their work. Over time, this leads to higher stress levels, burnout, and increased turnover, as employees seek workplaces where they are respected, trusted, and given opportunities to grow.

- Leadership Burnout: Micromanagers don't just harm their teams, they harm themselves. By taking on too many tasks that should be delegated, they spread themselves too thin, leading to stress, exhaustion, and decreased strategic focus. Instead of leading at a high level, they get bogged down in the details, unable to focus on long-term planning, vision, or leadership development.

The Power of Delegation

Effective leaders recognize that delegation is not a sign of weakness, it's a sign of trust and empowerment. Delegation allows leaders to focus on big-picture strategy, while also developing the skills and confidence of their teams. When leaders delegate properly, employees feel more invested in their work, take greater ownership of outcomes, and contribute more effectively to the organization's success.

Delegation benefits both leaders and employees in the following ways:

- Frees Up Leadership to Focus on Strategy: Leaders should be focused on vision, growth, and organizational success, not micromanaging daily tasks. By delegating, they create space to focus on high-level decisions, strategic initiatives, and leadership development.

- Developing Future Leaders: Effective delegation is an opportunity to mentor and train employees, preparing them for greater responsibilities and leadership roles. When employees are given autonomy and decision-making power, they build problem-solving skills, confidence, and leadership abilities.

- Boosts Team Morale and Engagement: Employees who are trusted with meaningful responsibilities feel more valued and motivated. They are more likely to contribute new ideas, take initiative, and feel ownership over their work, leading to higher engagement, creativity, and overall job satisfaction.

- Enhance Efficiency and Productivity: When leaders delegate appropriately, work gets done faster and more effectively. Teams can divide and conquer, rather than waiting for a leader to review every small detail. This enables organizations to move with greater agility and responsiveness.

How to Delegate Effectively

Delegation is an essential leadership skill—but it requires trust, clarity, and follow-through. Effective leaders don't just offload tasks, they set clear expectations, provide the necessary resources, and empower their teams to succeed. To delegate successfully:

- Assign the Right Tasks to the Right People: Understand your team's strengths, expertise, and growth potential. Delegate tasks to those who are best suited for them, or to those who can develop their skills through the opportunity.

- Communicate Clear Expectations: When delegating, provide clear instructions, objectives, and desired outcomes. Employees should understand what success looks like and have the resources needed to achieve it.

- Give Employees the Autonomy to Execute: Delegation does not mean micromanaging the process. Trust your employees to carry out their responsibilities without constant oversight. Provide guidance when needed but give them space to take ownership.

- Offer Support Without Taking Over: Be available for questions, feedback, or troubleshooting, but avoid the temptation to step in and "fix" things unless absolutely necessary. Empower employees to solve problems and make decisions on their own.

- Recognize and Reward Contributions: Acknowledge employees' efforts and successes. When leaders recognize strong performance and the ability to take on responsibility, employees feel motivated and confident to take on even bigger challenges.

Micromanagement is a leadership failure that stifles growth, innovation, and engagement. Leaders who fail to delegate and insist on controlling every aspect of operations create inefficiency, frustration, and ultimately, burnout—for both them and their teams.

In contrast, strong leaders embrace delegation as a tool for empowerment. They recognize that trusting their teams, providing clear direction, and allowing autonomy leads to stronger performance, higher engagement, and a more innovative workplace. True leadership is not about doing everything yourself, it's about developing those around you so that the organization can thrive beyond a single individual's efforts.

A leader who refuses to delegate is not leading—they are simply managing tasks. A leader who trusts, empowers, and builds others up creates a resilient, high-performing team capable of achieving more than anyone ever could alone. The question every leader must ask is: Am I enabling my team to grow, or am I holding them back by refusing to let go?

The Silent Killer of Growth

One of the most common yet damaging leadership failures is neglecting to invest in the development of employees. Many leaders make the mistake of believing that once an employee is hired, their skill set remains fixed—but this mindset creates stagnant teams with limited capacity for innovation, adaptability, and leadership succession. Without continuous learning, employees become disengaged, uninspired, and ultimately, unprepared for greater responsibilities.

Leaders who fail to provide mentorship, training, or growth opportunities not only weaken their teams but also jeopardize the long-term success of their organization. Without development programs, employees lack the tools to advance in their roles, contribute fresh ideas, or take on leadership positions when the need arises. This lack of progression creates a cycle of mediocrity, where employees remain at the same skill level while competitors innovate and move ahead.

Great leaders recognize that an organization's greatest asset is its people, and investing in their growth is critical to long-term success. They actively nurture talent, encourage continuous learning, and create clear pathways for career advancement. This includes providing mentorship, offering training programs, supporting skill development, and empowering employees to take on new challenges. When employees feel supported in their professional growth, they are more engaged, motivated, and committed to the organization's mission.

Strong leadership teams understand that developing employees is not an expense, it's an investment. The more an organization supports and builds its workforce, the more resilient, innovative, and competitive it becomes. Leaders who prioritize team development create loyal, skilled, and adaptable teams capable of driving success well into the future.

The Fastest Way to Ruin

Few leadership failures are as destructive as ethical breaches. Unethical leadership decisions don't just harm individuals within an organization; they can shatter reputations, destroy trust, and lead to catastrophic financial and legal consequences. Whether it's corporate fraud, exploitation, deception, or unethical labor practices, history is full of examples where scandals have brought down once-thriving companies and permanently tarnished their legacies.

When leaders prioritize personal gain, short-term profits, or unchecked power over integrity, they create a culture where dishonesty, manipulation, and unethical behavior thrive. Employees in such environments often feel pressured to cut corners, stay silent about wrongdoing, or engage in questionable practices to meet unrealistic goals. Over time, this erodes trust, weakens morale, and turns even high-performing organizations into breeding grounds for corruption.

The consequences of ethical failures are far-reaching. Public scandals alienate customers, investors, and business partners, often resulting in severe financial losses, legal penalties, and irreparable brand damage. Many companies that once dominated their industries have collapsed under the weight of their own unethical decisions. From high-profile fraud cases like Enron to companies exposed for exploitative labor practices, unethical leadership has a consistent track record of leading to disaster.

Strong leaders understand that ethics and accountability must be at the core of every decision. They set the tone for the entire organization, ensuring that transparency, honesty, and fairness are non-negotiable values. They don't just talk about integrity—they demonstrate it through their actions. When leaders operate with ethical clarity, they build trust, strengthen company culture, and create an environment where employees feel proud to contribute.

Integrity isn't just about avoiding scandals, it's about fostering a workplace culture where employees, stakeholders, and customers know they can trust leadership to do the right thing, even when no one is watching.

The Blind Spot That Kills Growth

Leaders who dismiss feedback from employees, customers, or stakeholders miss out on critical insights that could improve operations, drive innovation, and strengthen the organization. Leadership is not about having all the answers, it's about being willing to listen, learn, and adapt based on input from those closest to the work.

When leaders adopt a closed-off, authoritarian leadership style, they create a culture where employees feel unheard, customers feel undervalued, and innovation grinds to a halt. Without an open feedback loop, organizations risk making costly mistakes, repeating failures, and falling behind competitors who listen to their people and adapt accordingly.

A refusal to acknowledge feedback often stems from ego, fear of criticism, or the false belief that leadership is about commanding rather than learning. Leaders who ignore concerns or dismiss differing opinions ultimately create a disengaged workforce that stops speaking up. Employees either leave for organizations where their voices matter or become indifferent to workplace issues, further driving down morale and productivity.

In contrast, great leaders actively seek and incorporate feedback. They understand that constructive criticism is not a threat to authority but a tool for growth. They create a culture where employees feel valued, customers feel heard, and stakeholders know their input matters.

Effective leaders:

- Encourage honest dialogue by creating safe spaces for employees to share concerns without fear of retaliation.

- Actively solicit feedback through regular one-on-one meetings, surveys, and open forums.

- Use feedback as a learning tool, rather than viewing it as personal criticism.

- Demonstrate responsiveness by making meaningful improvements based on employee and customer insights.

When leaders embrace feedback rather than ignore it, they build a culture of continuous improvement, trust, and innovation. Employees become more engaged, customers become more loyal, and the organization as a whole benefits from smarter, more informed decision-making.

Ignoring feedback is not just a leadership weakness—it's a leadership blind spot that can lead to stagnation and failure. The best leaders understand that they don't need to have all the answers—they just need to be willing to listen and learn.

Case Studies of Leadership Failures

Leadership failures are not just theoretical concepts; they have played out in real-world scenarios, leading to the downfall of companies, missed opportunities, and lost market dominance. The following case studies highlight some of the most common leadership pitfalls—nepotism, poor hiring decisions, and resistance to change—and the consequences that followed.

Example 1: A Family-Owned Business Marred by Nepotism

One of the biggest risks in family-owned businesses is the temptation to prioritize personal relationships over merit. In one such case, a once-thriving manufacturing company slowly deteriorated due to favoritism in leadership selection. The company's founder, who had built the business from the ground up, chose to pass leadership to a family member rather than the most qualified individual for the role.

Despite concerns from senior employees and advisors, the new leader lacked both industry experience and the ability to manage complex operations. Rather than seeking guidance, they surrounded themselves with other family members and close friends, further limiting fresh perspectives and innovation. Over time, morale declined, top talent left the company, and internal conflicts increased as employees felt they had no opportunities for advancement unless they were part of the owner's inner circle.

Without strong, competent leadership, decision-making became erratic and reactive rather than strategic and forward-thinking. The company failed to keep up with industry trends, lost long-term clients, and ultimately succumbed to financial instability. What was once a market leader with decades of success crumbled due to leadership's failure to separate personal loyalty from professional competence.

Example 2: The Cost of Poor Hiring Decisions

Hiring the wrong leaders can be catastrophic for an organization, especially in a fast-moving industry. A promising tech startup, initially hailed as the next big disruptor, made a critical mistake when it rushed to fill key executive roles without proper vetting. The company's founders, eager to scale rapidly, prioritized filling leadership positions quickly rather than finding candidates with the right skills and cultural fit.

One of the most damaging hiring decisions involved appointing a CEO who had an impressive resume but lacked leadership qualities essential for the startup's high-pressure environment. Instead of fostering collaboration and inspiring innovation, the new leader micromanaged teams, discouraged open communication, and created a toxic workplace culture. Employees quickly became disengaged, and productivity plummeted.

Additionally, incompetent department heads were brought in without rigorous background checks, leading to poor financial decisions, failed marketing campaigns, and product mismanagement. The lack of a solid leadership foundation led to internal chaos, low investor confidence, and ultimately, the startup's collapse within just a few years. This case underscores the importance of hiring leaders based on qualifications, vision, and ability to inspire teams—not just an impressive resume or rapid expansion goals.

Example 3: Resistance to Technological Advancements

Failure to adapt to technological change has doomed many once-dominant companies, and the retail industry provides some of the most stunning examples of leadership failures in this area. A well-established retail giant, once a household name, found itself in rapid decline after failing to embrace e-commerce.

Despite clear market signals and the success of online retailers like Amazon, leadership dismissed digital transformation as a passing trend. Rather than investing in an online platform, upgrading supply chain logistics, or improving customer convenience through digital tools, the company doubled down on traditional brick-and-mortar sales strategies.

By the time the company finally acknowledged the need for an e-commerce presence, it was too late. Competitors had already secured market dominance, refined their digital operations, and built strong online customer loyalty. The retail giant suffered massive losses, was forced to close hundreds of stores, and eventually declared bankruptcy.

This case highlights a critical leadership lesson: Ignoring technological advancements is not just risky, it's a recipe for obsolescence. In today's rapidly evolving business landscape, leaders who resist change rather than embrace it will see their organizations fall behind and ultimately fail.

Example 4: Leadership Nepotism at a University

There is a University in Springfield, once a respected regional institution known for its strong academic programs and community engagement, faced a dramatic decline over a decade due to poor leadership choices driven by nepotism. What started as a promising institution began to unravel as top administrative positions were repeatedly filled by family members and close associates of the university president, rather than by the most qualified candidates.

The problems at this University began when the Board of Trustees appointed a new university president. Hastings had a long tenure at the institution but lacked experience in strategic planning and financial oversight. Shortly after taking office, he appointed his son as Vice President of Finance, despite having no experience in higher education finance. Around the same time, his brother-in-law, who had previously been a high school principal, was named Provost, responsible for overseeing academic affairs.

To make matters worse, this president favored hiring friends and family into key administrative roles, often bypassing formal hiring procedures. Over time, the leadership team became an insulated group of individuals more concerned with protecting each other than with making decisions that benefited the institution.

Financial Mismanagement & Declining Enrollment

The president, lacking expertise in university budgeting, made several poor financial decisions, including investing millions in a failing real estate venture meant to expand student housing. The project quickly became a money pit, diverting funds from crucial academic programs. Meanwhile, tuition continued to rise, leading to declining enrollment as students opted for more affordable alternatives.

Erosion of Faculty and Staff Morale

Under the nepotistic leadership, merit-based hiring and promotions were ignored. Instead of rewarding performance and experience, key faculty and administrative roles were given to personal acquaintances. Qualified faculty members were passed over for tenure in favor of friends of the administration, leading to widespread dissatisfaction. Over five years, faculty turnover increased by 45%, as talented professors left for institutions with fairer hiring practices.

Accreditation and Reputation Damage

The university's accreditation body raised concerns over declining academic standards and lack of transparent leadership. Auditors found that key administrators lacked the proper qualifications for their roles, and financial oversight was inadequate. As a result, the institution was placed on probation, leading to a significant loss of credibility and a further drop in student applications.

Student Impact and Legal Issues

The student body felt the impact of failed leadership through fewer course offerings, outdated resources, and a lack of career support services. Student complaints about mismanagement grew, and a lawsuit was eventually filed by faculty members claiming discriminatory hiring practices. This led to public scrutiny, negative media coverage, and increased pressure on the Board of Trustees.

The Collapse and Lessons Learned

By the time the Board of Trustees finally acted, the damage was irreversible. Facing public outcry and a dwindling budget, they removed the president and his close network from leadership, but the institution had already lost significant ground. The University struggled for years to recover and had to merge with another institution to remain operational.

This case highlights the dangers of nepotism in leadership, particularly in higher education, where decision-making must be driven by institutional mission rather than personal loyalty. This failure underscores the importance of merit-based leadership, transparency, and accountability to ensure the long-term success of any academic institution.

Key Takeaways from Leadership Failures

Each of these case studies demonstrates the long-term damage caused by poor leadership decisions. Whether nepotism leads to unqualified leadership, poor hiring choices destroying company culture, or resistance to change making an organization obsolete, the consequences are severe. These failures serve as powerful reminders that strong leadership requires foresight, adaptability, and a commitment to making tough but necessary decisions for the greater good of the organization.

The question every leader must ask is:

"Are my leadership choices setting my organization up for long-term success, or are they creating cracks that will eventually lead to collapse?"

The Legacy of Leadership—Failure or Greatness?

Leadership is not a position, it's a responsibility. It's not about titles, authority, or personal recognition, but about the impact you leave behind, the culture you create, and the people you inspire. True leadership is defined by continuous growth, self-awareness, and the courage to make the right decisions—even when they're the hardest ones to make.

History is filled with the wreckage of leaders who failed to adapt, refused to listen, or let their egos override wisdom. Organizations have crumbled because leaders resisted change, dismissed valuable feedback, or chose personal comfort over progress. The warning signs are always there—complacency, arrogance, unchecked control—but too often, leaders ignore them until it's too late. The downfall of failed leaders isn't usually one catastrophic mistake; it's a series of ignored red flags, small compromises, and missed opportunities to do better.

But failure is also a teacher—for those willing to learn, evolve, and rise above their past mistakes. The best leaders are not the ones who have never failed, but the ones who recognize their failures, adapt, and refuse to repeat them. They embrace accountability, seek out feedback, and remain open to new ideas, even when it challenges their own thinking. They know that leadership is not about control, it's about empowering others to succeed.

The real question is this: What kind of leader will you be? Will you be the leader who ignores the signs, dismisses dissenting voices, and clings to outdated methods until your organization collapses under your watch? Or will you be the leader who learns, grows, and makes the tough choices that lead to lasting success?

The legacy of leadership is to build one decision at a time. Make sure yours is one worth remembering.

Chapter 5

Cultivating a Leadership Pipeline

G reat leaderships are not accidental—it is intentional, developed, and cultivated over time. Organizations that fail to build a strong leadership pipeline find themselves scrambling when senior leaders retire, resign, or fail to meet expectations. Without a structured approach to identifying, training, and empowering future leaders, companies are left vulnerable to stagnation, high turnover, and uninspired management. However, the single biggest obstacle to building an effective leadership pipeline is nepotism and self-serving hiring practices. When leadership positions are filled based on personal relationships rather than competence, organizations sabotage their own potential for long-term success.

Cultivating a leadership pipeline is about proactively developing individuals who have the skills, mindset, and adaptability to step into leadership roles when the time comes. It is not just about filling positions, it's about ensuring that the next generation of leaders is stronger, more resilient, and more innovative than the last. But this is impossible when unqualified individuals are placed in leadership roles solely because of their connections. Instead of fostering growth and accountability, nepotism creates an insular leadership structure where critical decisions are made by those more interested in maintaining power than advancing the organization's mission.

This chapter explores the essential strategies for developing a leadership pipeline, including identifying and nurturing potential leaders, building resilience, fostering collaboration, promoting diversity and inclusion, and measuring success. Additionally, we examine the consequences of failed leadership development, particularly in cases where nepotism and agenda-driven hiring practices weaken an organization from within. Strong leadership isn't built on favoritism; it's built on identifying and elevating the best talent, ensuring the future of the organization is in the hands of those who can truly lead.

Identifying and Nurturing Potential Leaders

Leadership development does not begin at the moment of promotion, it starts long before that. Organizations must be proactive in identifying individuals with leadership potential and investing in their growth. Waiting until a leadership vacancy arises to begin searching for a suitable replacement often results in rushed, reactionary decision-making that may lead to underprepared leaders stepping into roles they are not equipped to handle. Instead, leadership development should be a continuous, intentional process that builds a strong pipeline of capable leaders who are ready to step up when the time comes.

Future leaders are not always the loudest voices in the room or those who naturally gravitate toward authority. Leadership potential is often found in individuals who demonstrate problem-solving abilities, strong emotional intelligence, and the ability to inspire others through action rather than words. These individuals are adaptable, thoughtful, and able to navigate complex challenges with a level-headed approach. To effectively develop future leaders, organizations must provide opportunities for mentorship, continuous learning, and hands-on leadership experience.

Implement Mentorship and Coaching Programs

One of the most effective ways to develop future leaders is through mentorship and coaching programs. By pairing emerging leaders with experienced mentors, organizations create an environment of knowledge transfer, guidance, and real-world insight that formal training alone cannot provide.

Mentorship allows experienced leaders to pass down lessons learned from their own careers, helping future leaders avoid common mistakes, develop strategic thinking skills, and gain confidence in decision-making. A strong mentorship culture fosters professional relationships, strengthens the organization's leadership structure, and ensures that valuable institutional knowledge is not lost when senior leaders retire or move on.

Coaching, on the other hand, provides a more structured, performance-driven approach to leadership development. Coaches work with emerging leaders to identify strengths, address weaknesses, and develop personalized strategies for growth. Unlike mentorship, which is often informal, coaching programs involve ongoing feedback, goal-setting, and regular progress reviews to ensure that leadership development stays on track.

A successful mentorship and coaching program creates a continuous cycle of leadership development, ensuring that each generation of leaders is stronger, more capable, and better prepared than the last.

Offer Leadership Training Workshops and Continuous Learning Opportunities

Leadership is not just a natural talent—it is a skill that must be continuously refined and developed. No leader is ever truly "finished" learning, as leadership demands adaptability, strategic thinking, and the ability to navigate constant change. To cultivate strong leaders, organizations must provide structured leadership development programs that offer both theoretical knowledge and practical application. However, leadership training should not be reduced to workshops held for the sake of appearances. Simply gathering employees in a room to check a training box is a waste of time and resources. True leadership development comes from meaningful, hands-on training that equips individuals with the skills they need to lead effectively.

Effective leadership training should include:

- Workshops with Purpose: Training sessions should be designed to develop key leadership skills, such as conflict resolution, decision-making, strategic planning, and emotional intelligence—not just to fulfill a requirement.
- Formal Leadership Development Courses: Employees should have access to structured programs that help them understand the responsibilities, challenges, and expectations of leadership roles.
- Real-World Application: Exposure to real challenges through case studies, simulations, and hands-on projects ensures that leaders are prepared to navigate the complexities of running an organization.

Additionally, learning should not stop after an individual is promoted into a leadership role. Continuous education through executive coaching, peer learning groups, and advanced leadership courses helps leaders stay sharp, adaptable, and prepared to tackle new challenges. Organizations that invest in substantive, ongoing leadership education—rather than superficial training exercise ensure that their leaders remain ahead of industry trends and are equipped to drive innovation and change.

Encourage Proactive Leadership Experience

The fastest way to develop leadership skills is to give individuals opportunities to lead. Theoretical training is valuable, but nothing can replace real-world experience. Organizations must be deliberate about creating opportunities for employees to take on leadership responsibilities, even in small ways.

One effective approach is to offer stretch assignments—projects or roles that challenge employees to step beyond their comfort zones. These assignments allow emerging leaders to develop critical thinking skills, build confidence, and gain hands-on experience managing teams, solving problems, and making decisions.

Temporary leadership roles, such as serving as an interim team leader, heading a special project, or managing a cross-functional initiative, provide valuable real-world leadership exposure without the long-term commitment of an official promotion. These opportunities allow individuals to test their leadership capabilities, identify areas for improvement, and learn from their experiences in a supportive environment.

Additionally, encouraging cross-functional project management enables potential leaders to develop a broader understanding of the organization, strengthen collaboration skills, and learn how to manage teams with diverse expertise and perspectives. This is especially important for future senior leaders who will need to navigate complex interdepartmental challenges.

By systematically identifying, nurturing, and giving emerging leaders opportunities to lead, organizations create a steady pipeline of skilled individuals who are prepared to take on greater responsibilities when the need arises.

The Long-Term Impact of Leadership Development

Developing strong leaders is not a short-term initiative, it is a long-term investment in the future success of an organization. Without a clear and proactive leadership development strategy, organizations risk stagnation, high turnover, and uncertainty in leadership transitions. However, when mentorship, continuous learning, and real-world leadership opportunities are prioritized, organizations cultivate a strong, confident, and capable leadership pipeline that ensures stability, innovation, and long-term success.

The best organizations do not wait until they have a leadership vacancy to start searching for a replacement—they are always developing, refining, and strengthening their next generation of leaders. The question is not whether you have future leaders in your organization, but the question is whether you are actively preparing them for success.

Building Resilience and Agility

Leadership is not just about making great decisions when times are good, it is about navigating crises, leading through uncertainty, and remaining steadfast under pressure. The most effective leaders are those who can think clearly in chaotic situations, adapt to unexpected challenges, and maintain a sense of direction even when the path ahead is unclear. However, resilience and agility are not inherent traits; they must be developed and reinforced through intentional leadership training. Future leaders must be trained to handle stress, make high-pressure decisions, and pivot when necessary.

One of the most effective ways to build resilience is to teach future leaders how to manage crises and thrive under pressure. Leadership training programs should include crisis simulations, scenario planning, and case studies of high-stakes decision-making. By exposing leaders to realistic, high-pressure situations in a controlled learning environment, organizations can help them develop confidence, problem-solving abilities, and decision-making skills necessary to lead effectively in difficult times. These exercises prepare leaders to remain composed, think strategically, and act decisively when faced with adversity.

Another crucial component of resilience is emotional strength and stress management. Even the most talented leaders can be derailed by burnout, emotional fatigue, and chronic stress. Organizations must prioritize training future leaders on stress management techniques, mindfulness practices, and strategies for maintaining emotional balance in high-pressure environments. Leaders who understand how to manage their stress are better equipped to support their teams, make rational decisions, and sustain their energy over the long term.

Resilient leaders are those who can weather storms, pivot when necessary, and maintain clarity and focus in moments of uncertainty. Organizations that actively develop resilience in their leadership teams ensure that their future leaders will not only survive in volatile environments but thrive in them. By fostering a leadership culture that values adaptability, emotional intelligence, and strategic problem-solving, companies equip their future leaders with the tools to navigate the evolving challenges of the business world with confidence and agility.

Fostering a Culture of Collaboration

Leadership is not a solo act; it's a team effort; far too often forgotten is this basic concept. The most successful organizations do not rely on individual leaders operating in isolation, but rather on leadership teams that work together, share insights, and align their efforts toward common goals. A strong leadership pipeline must prioritize collaboration, cross-functional teamwork, and shared decision-making to ensure that leaders at all levels are equipped to work across departments, break down silos, and drive organizational success collectively.

One key aspect of fostering collaboration is to encourage teamwork and cross-functional collaboration. Leaders should be trained to work across different departments, bridge gaps between teams, and build relationships that extend beyond their immediate roles. When leaders understand how different areas of the organization contribute to the bigger picture, they can make more informed decisions and foster a culture of cooperation rather than competition. A leadership pipeline that emphasizes cross-functional exposure ensures that future leaders are well-rounded and able to navigate complex, multi-departmental challenges.

Additionally, shared decision-making and collective problem-solving must be core components of leadership training. Great leaders do not dictate, they empower teams to contribute ideas, challenge assumptions, and collaborate on solutions. Leadership development programs should emphasize how to balance authority with inclusivity, teaching leaders how to listen actively, encourage participation, and create an environment where diverse perspectives drive innovation. When leadership is built on collective intelligence rather than individual dominance, organizations become more resilient, adaptable, and forward-thinking.

To strengthen collaboration, organizations should incorporate team-building activities into leadership development programs. Future leaders should participate in leadership retreats, structured problem-solving exercises, and group challenges designed to build trust and cohesion. A cohesive leadership team operates with transparency, shared vision, and mutual respect, all of which are critical for maintaining a healthy, high-performing organization.

A leadership pipeline that fosters collaboration rather than hierarchy creates a more dynamic, engaged, and adaptable workforce. By prioritizing teamwork, encouraging shared decision-making, and building strong interpersonal relationships among leaders, organizations set the stage for long-term success, innovation, and a culture where leadership is not about individual power, but about collective progress.

Diversity, Equity, and Inclusion in Leadership

A leadership team that lacks diversity lacks perspective. Organizations that prioritize inclusivity in leadership development foster more innovative, forward-thinking, and culturally competent teams. When leaders come from varied backgrounds and experiences, they bring unique problem-solving approaches and fresh perspectives, ultimately driving better decision-making and stronger organizational outcomes. However, diversity, equity, and inclusion (DEI) efforts should enhance an organization, not hinder it. DEI should be a tool for strengthening leadership selection and creating equal opportunities, not a justification for lowering hiring standards or placing organizational success at risk. The goal of DEI is to improve the system, not compromise the quality of leadership decisions.

To build a leadership pipeline that truly reflects diversity, organizations must ensure potential leaders come from diverse backgrounds. The most innovative ideas emerge from teams that represent a wide range of experiences and viewpoints, helping organizations adapt to changing markets, customer needs, and global business trends. Leadership training programs should be accessible to employees across different career paths, backgrounds, and disciplines to ensure that leadership opportunities are open to all who demonstrate capability and potential.

At the same time, inclusive hiring and promotion practices must be based on merit, not politics or favoritism. Bias in leadership selection—whether based on personal relationships, outdated stereotypes, or unchecked assumptions—can prevent the most capable individuals from rising to leadership roles. Organizations must establish transparent, objective criteria for leadership development and promotions, ensuring that every candidate is evaluated based on skills, achievements, and potential rather than superficial characteristics.

Additionally, organizations should address unconscious bias through training and awareness programs. Many leadership failures stem from hiring in one's own image (i.e. *who you see in the mirror*), where leaders unintentionally favor candidates who think, act, or look like them rather than selecting individuals who bring fresh ideas and diverse perspectives. Unconscious bias training helps organizations recognize and counteract these tendencies, allowing them to build leadership teams that truly reflect the workforce, customer base, and community they serve.

A diverse leadership team is not just a moral obligation, it is a business advantage. Studies show that companies with diverse leadership teams outperform their competitors in innovation, employee satisfaction, and overall performance. A leadership pipeline that prioritizes diversity without sacrificing quality ensures that organizations remain competitive, resilient, and equipped to tackle modern challenges with a broader, more inclusive perspective. The key is balance—DEI should elevate the organization, ensuring that diversity enhances leadership rather than becoming an exercise of checking a box that weakens long-term success.

Measuring Leadership Development Success

A leadership pipeline is only effective if it produces measurable results. Organizations cannot simply assume that leadership development programs are working; they must track progress, assess effectiveness, and refine strategies based on real data. Without clear performance metrics, organizations risk investing time and resources into programs that do not yield strong, capable leaders.

To ensure effectiveness, organizations should define clear metrics to assess leadership program success. These metrics may include retention rates, promotion success, employee satisfaction scores, and leadership readiness evaluations. By tracking these indicators, organizations can identify strengths and weaknesses in their leadership pipeline and make data-driven improvements.

Another key tool for assessing leadership development is 360-degree feedback and regular performance reviews. Gathering insights from employees, peers, and mentors provides a well-rounded evaluation of a leader's growth, influence, and effectiveness. Honest feedback helps identify blind spots, strengths, and areas that require additional development. Leaders who receive constructive feedback regularly are more likely to refine their skills, improve communication, and enhance team engagement.

Finally, organizations must continuously refine leadership development strategies based on measurable outcomes. The business landscape is constantly evolving, and leadership training must keep pace with new challenges, emerging skills, and shifting industry trends. What worked five years ago may no longer be effective today. Leadership development programs should be regularly reviewed, updated, and adapted to ensure they remain relevant, impactful, and aligned with the organization's long-term goals.

Strong leadership development programs are dynamic, not static. Organizations that measure, adapt, and refine their leadership pipeline will not only stay competitive but also cultivate leaders who are truly prepared to drive success in an ever-changing world.

Failed Hires and Agenda-Driven Leadership Failures

Not all leadership development efforts succeed, some fail due to personal biases, political agendas, and short-sighted decision-making. Poor leadership selection can erode organizational confidence, stifle innovation, and lead to long-term uncertainty. The following common mistakes undermine leadership development and can have lasting negative consequences:

- One of the biggest mistakes organizations make is prioritizing personal connections over competence. Some select leaders based on friendships, personal alliances, or loyalty rather than on actual qualifications and leadership ability. This results in ineffective leadership, internal resentment, and a workforce that feels overlooked in favor of personal favoritism. When leaders are chosen based on who they know rather than what they bring to the table, the organization suffers from weak decision-making, lack of direction, and an overall decline in performance.

- Another common failure is disregarding development programs. Some leaders skip mentorship, training, and development opportunities because they believe their charisma, connections, or reputation will be enough to succeed. However, leadership is not just about presence, it requires critical thinking, adaptability, and strategic decision-making. Leaders who fail to invest in their own development often lack the necessary skills to navigate complex challenges, inspire their teams, or drive organizational growth.

- A particularly damaging mistake is enabling echo chambers within leadership teams. When organizations only hire leaders who share their viewpoints and dismiss those who challenge or offer different perspectives, they create a stagnant culture that resists change, innovation, and progress. Strong leadership thrives on diverse perspectives, open dialogue, and the ability to consider multiple viewpoints before making key decisions. A lack of diversity in thought leads to groupthink, missed opportunities, and an organization that falls behind competitors who embrace fresh ideas.

Poor leadership selection results in frustration, disengagement, and organizational decline. Organizations that fail to prioritize merit-based leadership development ultimately create unstable work environments, lose valuable talent, and weaken their ability to compete in the marketplace. Building a strong leadership pipeline requires discipline, transparency, and a commitment to selecting, developing, and promoting leaders based on capability—not personal relationships or political motivations.

Building A Legacy That Endures

A successful leadership pipeline is not built overnight, it is deliberately cultivated through vision, discipline, and long-term investment. Leadership development is not a checkbox task or a one-time initiative; it is the foundation upon which sustainable success is built. Organizations that prioritize leadership development today ensure that they have strong, capable leaders prepared to take on the uncertainties of tomorrow.

But true leadership is not just about holding positions of authority, it is about creating a ripple effect of growth, mentorship, and empowerment. The best leaders don't just lead, they create new leaders. They identify potential, foster resilience, champion collaboration, and build a culture where leadership is not hoarded but multiplied. By investing in people, embracing diversity of thought, and consistently measuring progress, organizations don't just prepare for the future, they shape it.

The defining question for every organization is this: Are we merely filling leadership roles for today, or are we cultivating the visionaries, problem-solvers, and changemakers who will define the future? The organizations that get this right will not just survive the evolving business landscape; they will thrive, innovate, and lead it.

"True leadership is not about holding power—it's about empowering others to lead, breaking down silos, and building a legacy of collaboration, innovation, and trust that endures beyond any single individual"

Chapter 6

The Leaderless Leader

Leadership is often associated with strength, decisiveness, and vision. However, one of the most damaging forms of leadership failure is not overt incompetence or authoritarian control, but the absence of leadership altogether. This phenomenon, known as leaderless leadership, occurs when someone in a leadership position fails to make decisions, provide guidance, or take responsibility for the success or failures of their team. While they may hold the title of a leader, their actions—or lack thereof—create a vacuum where teams are left without clear direction, critical decisions are stalled, and overall productivity suffers.

A leaderless leader is not simply an ineffective manager; they actively avoid the very responsibilities that define strong leadership. They delegate excessively without accountability, shift responsibilities to others without providing necessary support, and hesitate when decisions need to be made. Instead of providing a vision for their team, they remain passive, indecisive, and disconnected, leaving employees unsure of priorities and expectations. Without a guiding force, teams lose momentum, lack motivation, and struggle to function cohesively.

Characteristics of a Leaderless Leader

At first glance, a leaderless leader may not seem as problematic as an openly toxic or dictatorial leader, but the consequences of their inaction can be just as damaging, if not worse. Unlike an openly destructive leader, whose faults are often obvious and eventually addressed, the leaderless leader operates in a fog of incompetence disguised as ambition, creating dysfunction that spreads through an organization slowly, often unnoticed until significant damage has been done. These individuals lack vision, direction, and the ability to inspire their teams, leaving employees to operate in a state of ambiguity and uncertainty. Without a clear mission, defined goals, or strategic direction, teams become fragmented and unaligned, unsure of where their efforts should be focused, ultimately leading to stagnation, low morale, and disorganization.

What makes a leaderless leader even more insidious is that they are often the loudest voices in the room when leadership opportunities arise. They will run, beg, and campaign for any and all leadership positions, regardless of whether they are qualified, experienced, or capable of handling the responsibilities. To them, leadership is not about guiding a team, making strategic decisions, or driving meaningful change, it is about holding the title of "leader." They crave prestige, the power, and the validation that comes with a leadership position, yet when they secure these roles, they fail to lead in any meaningful way. Instead of focusing on the success of their teams, their priority remains securing their title, maintaining their position, and ensuring they are recognized as "leaders" even if they contribute nothing of substance.

A leaderless leader is also reluctant to address conflicts, preferring to avoid difficult conversations rather than confront challenges head-on. They do not want to risk upsetting employees, making unpopular decisions, or being held responsible for outcomes. Instead of resolving disputes, setting expectations, or making tough calls, they allow problems to linger, hoping they will resolve themselves or that someone else will step in to fix them. This absence of accountability creates a tense and dysfunctional work environment, where issues remain unaddressed, resentment builds, and employees lose faith in leadership altogether. Over time, this breeds a toxic culture of avoidance, where no one takes responsibility, difficult conversations are indefinitely postponed, and employees become disengaged and frustrated.

Perhaps most critically, these leaders struggle with decision-making. They do not want the burden of making tough choices, preferring instead to delay, deflect, or push responsibility onto others. Even in moments that demand decisive action, they hesitate, weigh every possible consequence to an obsessive degree, and ultimately do nothing. Instead of guiding their teams, they create paralysis—bottlenecks emerge, initiatives stall, and employees are left floundering in uncertainty. Delegation, which is an essential leadership skill, is taken to an extreme and unproductive level—responsibilities are offloaded to subordinates without direction, oversight, or accountability. The result is confusion, inefficiency, and repeated failures, as no one is truly sure who is responsible for key initiatives. Employees feel unsupported, unmotivated, and disillusioned, realizing that while their leader holds the title, they lack the will or competence to actually lead.

Ultimately, a leaderless leader is a master of appearance but a failure in execution. They campaign aggressively for leadership roles, seek titles at any cost, and revel in the prestige of authority—yet when the moment comes to act, they falter, defer, and disappear into the background. The damage they inflict is not always immediately apparent, but over time, their inaction cripples teams, weakens morale, and erodes organizational trust. Leadership is not about holding a title, it is about responsibility, action, and accountability. A leader who does nothing is no leader at all.

Organizational Impact

The absence of strong leadership does not simply create minor inconvenience, it sends shockwaves throughout an organization, undermining morale, productivity, and long-term success. A leaderless leader is not just a neutral figurehead, they actively weaken the structure of the organization by failing to establish direction, align priorities, or make critical decisions. Teams under a leaderless leader often become directionless, operating without a clear strategy or defined purpose. Employees are left to navigate uncertainty without guidance, unsure of what is expected of them or how their work contributes to larger goals. Without leadership to unify efforts, establish priorities, and provide a vision, employees become disengaged, uninspired, and unmotivated, leading to a sharp decline in both efficiency and innovation.

One of the most serious consequences of leaderless leadership is delayed decision-making. Organizations rely on leadership to set objectives, approve strategies, and take decisive action—when leaders fail to take responsibility, projects stall, opportunities are missed, and progress grinds to a halt. Instead of driving growth and innovation, the organization drifts aimlessly, unable to adapt to industry shifts or seize new possibilities. Companies that lack strong, decisive leadership struggle to respond to market changes, adjust strategies in competitive environments, and address internal challenges before they escalate. This lack of adaptability puts them at a significant disadvantage, allowing more dynamic, well-led competitors to overtake them. Over time, the organization's culture begins to erode, as employees lose faith in leadership, disengage from their work, and develop a sense of futility about their contributions.

Perhaps one of the most frustrating realities is that the leaderless leader is often the most vocal advocate for leadership titles. They campaign relentlessly, positioning themselves as the perfect candidate for leadership positions, despite lacking the vision, competence, or courage to actually lead. They demand recognition, authority, and influence, but when granted leadership, they wield power in a way that paralyzes the organization rather than strengthens it. Their need for status outweighs their ability to fulfill the role, leading to a crisis of confidence among employees who recognize that their so-called leader is unable or unwilling to take decisive action. This not only undermines workplace morale but can also create resentment, as employees watch capable individuals passed over in favor of someone whose only qualification is persistence in demanding a title.

Employee morale is deeply affected by leaderless leadership. People want to feel supported, valued, and guided by those in charge. When leadership is absent, employees begin to question their roles, feel disconnected from the organization's mission, and lose confidence in their own contributions. Without a clear vision or direction, employees start to feel that their work lacks meaning, leading to higher turnover, increased frustration, and a decline in overall workplace satisfaction. This creates a revolving door of talent, where strong performers either leave in search of better leadership or disengage, reducing their contributions to the organization.

Without a strong leader to set expectations, provide feedback, and drive performance, teams struggle to stay motivated and engaged. Productivity suffers, collaboration weakens, and an unspoken culture of apathy spreads through the organization. Employees stop pushing boundaries, taking initiative, or offering creative solutions because they know that leadership will not act on their ideas or provide the necessary support to implement them. Over time, the organization becomes a hollow shell, operating out of habit rather than innovation, and surviving rather than thriving.

The leaderless leader is not just a harmless figurehead; they actively destabilize the organization, creating an environment where uncertainty reigns, morale collapses, and progress comes to a standstill. Their presence in leadership is not just ineffective, it is actively destructive. The damage caused by their inaction can take years to reverse, as trust must be rebuilt, engagement must be reignited, and organizational culture must be restored. A leader who refuses to lead is worse than no leader at all, because they occupy a space where real leadership should exist but fail to fulfill its most fundamental responsibilities.

Root Causes of Leaderless Leadership

Leaderless leadership is not always the result of sheer incompetence or a lack of ambition. In many cases, it arises from deep-rooted fears, structural deficiencies, or a failure to properly prepare individuals for leadership roles. While it may be easy to label a leaderless leader as ineffective or unqualified, the reality is often more complex, shaped by psychological barriers, systemic failures, and organizational complacency.

"Indecision is the silent killer of success—while leaders hesitate, opportunities vanish, morale crumbles, and the competition moves forward"

One of the primary reasons leaders become ineffective is a fear of failure or criticism. Many individuals in leadership positions become paralyzed by the weight of responsibility, overwhelmed by the pressure to make the right decisions, satisfy stakeholders, and manage team expectations simultaneously. Instead of embracing the role of decision-maker, they default to avoidance, deflection, or endless deliberation. Every choice feels like a potential risk, every action an opportunity for scrutiny—so instead of acting, they stall. This fear stifles progress, delays key initiatives, and fosters an environment where inaction becomes the norm rather than the exception. Over time, this avoidance erodes confidence in leadership, as employees and peers begin to recognize that decisions are either being pushed aside indefinitely or outsourced to others without clear direction.

"A company without decisive leadership is like a ship without a captain—adrift, directionless, and destined to sink"

Another significant contributor to leaderless leadership is a lack of training or experience. Many individuals rise through the ranks due to their technical expertise rather than their leadership ability, meaning that by the time they are placed in positions of authority, they are ill-equipped to manage people, communicate expectations, or make difficult decisions. They may excel as subject-matter experts, but leading a team requires a vastly different skill set—one that they were never formally taught. Without adequate leadership development, mentorship, or real-world experience in managing teams, these individuals flounder in their roles, struggling to establish authority or build trust with their teams. Conflict resolution becomes an insurmountable challenge, delegation feels like a loss of control, and decision-making is either hesitant or inconsistent. Faced with these challenges, many retreat into passivity, allowing their teams to operate in a state of uncertainty rather than addressing their leadership gaps head-on.

"Failing to make a decision is still a decision—one that fuels uncertainty, weakens morale, and invites failure."

Beyond individual fears and lack of preparation, organizational culture can actively reinforce leaderless leadership by allowing passive behaviors to persist unchecked. In some companies, weak accountability structures, ineffective performance evaluations, and outdated hierarchies create an environment where passive leadership is tolerated—even rewarded. If there are no real consequences for failing to lead, no benchmarks for evaluating leadership effectiveness, and no clear feedback mechanisms to identify leadership deficiencies, then leaderless leaders will continue to occupy key positions indefinitely. In such organizations, employees may grow accustomed to a culture of inertia, where decisions are endlessly deferred, initiatives stagnate, and leadership remains an abstract concept rather than an active force.

"Success demands action. When leaders refuse to decide, they don't just stall progress, they hand failure the keys to the organization."

Organizations that fail to recognize and address the damage caused by absent leadership often find themselves trapped in cycles of stagnation and disengagement, unable to break free from ineffective management structures. Without a commitment to leadership development, accountability, and proactive decision-making, the presence of leaderless leaders will continue to sap organizational momentum, weaken employee morale, and hinder overall success. The consequences of passive leadership are not immediate explosions of failure—they are slow, creeping declines that erode a company's ability to compete, innovate, and retain top talent. A company does not need an openly toxic leader to fail—it only needs a leader who refuses to lead.

Turning Passive Leadership into Proactive Leadership

To combat the damaging effects of leaderless leadership, organizations must take deliberate and sustained action to develop, support, and hold leaders accountable for their roles. Leadership is not a passive title, it is an active responsibility that requires continuous growth, clear expectations, and a commitment to making impactful decisions. Without structured efforts to transform ineffective leadership, organizations risk falling into cycles of stagnation, disengagement, and poor performance.

"Proactive leadership isn't about reacting to problems, it's about anticipating them, staying ahead of the curve, and turning challenges into opportunities."

One of the most effective solutions is to provide targeted leadership development and coaching to help struggling leaders gain confidence, improve decision-making, and strengthen their ability to guide teams effectively. Many leaderless leaders are not inherently incapable—they are simply unprepared for the complexities of leadership, having been promoted based on technical expertise rather than their ability to manage people. Leadership training should not be generic—it must be tailored to address the specific challenges these individuals face, focusing on strategic thinking, conflict resolution, and effective communication. Training programs should be interactive and practical, incorporating real-world scenarios, mentorship, and hands-on leadership exercises to ensure that leaders develop the skills necessary to step into their roles with authority and clarity.

"The best leaders don't wait for success to happen; they create it through vision, strategy, and decisive action."

However, training alone is not enough. Organizations must establish clear expectations and accountability structures to ensure that leadership is not just a title but an ongoing responsibility. Leaders must know exactly what is expected of them, with clearly defined roles, performance benchmarks, and measurable leadership goals. Too often, organizations assume that once someone reaches a leadership position, they will instinctively know how to perform—but without structured accountability, even well-intentioned leaders can become complacent, avoidant, or overwhelmed. Performance expectations must be regularly reinforced through leadership evaluations, goal-setting sessions, and structured leadership development plans. By creating a leadership culture that values action, decisiveness, and accountability, organizations ensure that leaders step up rather than fade into the background.

"Proactive leadership builds momentum, inspires confidence, and transforms potential into lasting success."

Encouraging feedback from teams is another essential step in identifying and addressing leadership gaps before they become major problems. Employees are often the first to recognize when leadership is ineffective, absent, or disengaged. However, many organizations lack safe and transparent channels for employees to express concerns about leadership performance. Without an avenue for honest feedback, passive leaders remain unchecked, and employee frustrations simmer beneath the surface until they lead to disengagement, turnover, or widespread dissatisfaction.

"Organizations thrive when leaders take charge, make bold decisions, and guide their teams with clarity and purpose."

To counter this, organizations must implement a system of continuous leadership evaluation, using regular performance reviews, anonymous feedback surveys, and one-on-one discussions to gauge whether leaders are effectively guiding their teams or simply occupying a position of power. Leadership feedback should not be seen as a punitive measure— rather, it should be a tool for growth, helping leaders understand their weaknesses, refine their strengths, and make meaningful improvements. By acting on feedback rather than dismissing it, organizations create a culture of transparency and continuous improvement, where leaders are not just held accountable but are actively supported in their journey to becoming stronger, more effective figures within the company.

"A great leader takes responsibility for failure, gives credit in success, and never shifts the blame, because true leadership is about owning the outcome, not just the title."

Ultimately, turning passive leadership into proactive leadership requires a combination of training, accountability, and open communication. Organizations that fail to address leaderless leadership will struggle with disengagement, inefficiency, and stalled progress. However, by actively developing their leadership teams, enforcing accountability measures, and creating transparent feedback loops, companies can foster a culture of strong, decisive leadership that drives long-term success. Leadership should never be a position of convenience; it should be a responsibility that demands action, commitment, and the willingness to evolve in service of the team and the organization.

The consequences of leaderless leadership are not hypothetical—they have played out in real-world organizations, resulting in significant business failures, internal dysfunction, and cultural decay. Companies that failed to hold leaders accountable for decision-making and strategic guidance have seen entire departments collapse due to inaction and uncertainty. Case studies from various industries demonstrate the dangers of passive leadership and the importance of decisive, engaged leaders.

For example, in a struggling tech startup, a passive CEO refused to make necessary restructuring decisions, fearing backlash from employees and investors. As a result, the company ran out of cash, failed to pivot in time, and ultimately folded due to its leader's unwillingness to act. In another case, a retail giant suffered a slow decline after the upper management avoided addressing internal inefficiencies, leading to years of mismanagement and dwindling market share. These cases serve as a warning about the dangers of inaction and emphasize the critical role of strong leadership in driving organizational success.

The Hidden Cost of Leaderless Leadership

Leaderless leadership is not an obvious explosion of failure, it is a slow, corrosive decay that eats away at an organization from the inside out. It creates confusion, stagnation, and frustration, often creeping into a company's culture long before the true damage is recognized. Teams drift without direction, decisions stall until opportunities pass, and morale erodes as employees lose faith in leadership that refuses to lead. By the time organizations fully grasp the extent of the problem, they may find themselves crippled by disengagement, inefficiency, and an exodus of top talent seeking leadership elsewhere.

Leadership is not just a title, it is an action, a responsibility, and a commitment to clarity, decisiveness, and accountability. Without these qualities, leadership ceases to exist, leaving behind only empty authority, unchecked indecision, and a culture of passive dysfunction. The failure to confront leaderless leadership is not just a missed opportunity, it is a direct path to long-term failure, as organizations that tolerate passive leadership ultimately invite their own decline.

But the organizations that recognize and correct leaderless leadership early are the ones that will thrive. They will replace indecision with action, avoidance with accountability, and stagnation with momentum. They will build a culture where leadership is not just a title but a force that propels teams forward, drives innovation, and inspires confidence. Leadership is meant to ignite progress, not extinguish it—and the difference between an organization that rises or collapses lies in its willingness to ensure that every leader, at every level, truly leads.

"A leader who avoids decisions and accountability isn't just neutral—they are a silent force of destruction, eroding trust, stalling progress, and creating a culture of inaction that suffocates success"

Chapter 7

The Future of Leadership

Leadership is evolving at a pace never seen before. The traditional, top-down approach is rapidly being replaced by dynamic, adaptable, and purpose-driven leadership models that emphasize innovation, ethical responsibility, and technological integration. In a world where remote work, artificial intelligence, and social accountability shape the corporate landscape, today's leaders must be more than decision-makers; they must be visionaries. The leaders of the future will not be those who simply react to change but those who anticipate and drive it. As organizations continue to face technological disruptions, shifting workforce demographics, and heightened expectations for ethical leadership, the ability to navigate complexity with agility and purpose has never been more critical.

The Role of Technology

Technology has redefined what it means to lead in the modern era. Artificial intelligence, big data, and automation have become indispensable tools for decision-making, allowing leaders to move beyond intuition and base strategies on real-time insights. In a world where industries evolve rapidly, the ability to analyze trends, predict market shifts, and optimize operations with data-driven precision provides organizations with a competitive edge. From predictive analytics guiding business strategies to AI-driven performance evaluations identifying top talent, leaders now have access to an unprecedented level of information that enhances efficiency, reduces risk, and maximizes outcomes.

However, as technology grows more sophisticated, leaders face a significant challenge: balancing innovation with the human element. While AI can process vast amounts of data, detect patterns, and streamline operations, it lacks emotional intelligence, creativity, and ethical reasoning—qualities that are essential to effective leadership. Over-reliance on algorithms and automation risks creating impersonal workplaces where employees feel like mere numbers rather than valued contributors. Successful leaders must integrate technology into their leadership approach without losing sight of human experience. This means using AI as an augmentation tool rather than a replacement for critical thinking, empathy, and interpersonal relationships.

Beyond decision-making, technology has also reshaped the very structure of work itself. The rise of remote and hybrid workforces has transformed leadership dynamics, making virtual leadership a necessary skill for the modern executive. Managing a decentralized workforce requires more than just technological proficiency, it demands an entirely new leadership mindset. Leaders must cultivate trust, engagement, and cohesion among teams that may never meet in person. This includes leveraging collaboration platforms like Slack, Microsoft Teams, and Zoom to facilitate communication, setting clear expectations for remote productivity, and ensuring that employees remain connected to the organization's mission and culture despite physical distance.

Moreover, the digital transformation of leadership extends beyond internal operations to external communication and brand management. In an era where social media and digital engagement shape public perception, leaders must be mindful of their online presence, transparency, and responsiveness. A single misstep in the digital realm—whether through a poorly worded tweet or an AI-driven customer service failure—can have significant reputational consequences. Leaders must navigate this landscape with a keen awareness of how technology amplifies both opportunities and risks.

The future of leadership will be defined by those who can seamlessly integrate technology into their strategies while maintaining the core principles of human connection, ethical responsibility, and adaptability. The best leaders will not only harness the power of AI, automation, and data analytics but also recognize that the heart of any organization lies in its people. Technology should empower, not replace, the qualities that make great leaders: vision, empathy, creativity, and integrity.

Ethical Leadership in a Globalized World

In an era where social and environmental responsibility can no longer be ignored, ethical leadership has become a cornerstone of sustainable success. Consumers, employees, investors, and regulators now demand greater accountability from organizations, expecting them to take clear and decisive stances on critical issues such as climate change, diversity, labor rights, and corporate governance. Companies that fail to meet these expectations risk losing trust, market share, and long-term viability. The future leader must be one who not only acknowledges these responsibilities but actively integrates them into decision-making processes, ensuring that ethical considerations are not just corporate buzzwords but core operational principles.

Ethical leadership extends beyond compliance with regulations; it requires a proactive approach to corporate responsibility. Leaders must make decisions that align not only with financial goals but also with long-term societal and environmental well-being. This means taking meaningful action to reduce carbon footprints, ensuring fair and inclusive workplaces, and upholding high standards of corporate integrity. Companies that genuinely commit to these principles are rewarded with customer loyalty, stronger employee engagement, and enhanced brand reputation, while those that engage in performative activism, making empty promises without concrete actions, quickly find themselves exposed in the court of public opinion.

Demand for Transparency

One of the new buzzwords of the times is, Transparency, and it is said over and over again each day. With the rapid spread of information through digital media and investigative journalism, the public can scrutinize leadership decisions in real time. Social media platforms, whistleblower reports, and independent watchdog organizations ensure that unethical behavior—whether in the form of exploitative labor practices, environmental harm, or financial misconduct—rarely remains hidden for long. Leaders who attempt to deceive stakeholders, manipulate data, or hide corporate wrongdoing often face severe consequences, from reputational damage to legal repercussions.

Companies that embrace transparency, on the other hand, foster trust and long-term credibility. Ethical leaders understand that trust is built not through polished press releases but through consistent, authentic actions. This means openly addressing challenges, admitting mistakes, and demonstrating a commitment to continuous improvement. Businesses that communicate their ethical commitments clearly—and follow through on them are more likely to attract top talent, retain customers, and maintain positive stakeholder relationships.

Business Case for Ethical Leadership

Beyond moral obligation, ethical leadership is also a smart business strategy. Studies have consistently shown that companies with strong ethical foundations outperform their competitors in the long run. Investors increasingly use environmental, social, and governance (ESG) metrics to assess the sustainability and ethical standing of a company before committing capital. Employees, particularly the younger generations, seek workplaces that align with their personal values, making ethical leadership a key factor in talent attraction and retention.

Moreover, businesses that engage in ethical practices are more resilient in times of crisis. Organizations that have built a foundation of trust and accountability are better equipped to navigate market downturns, regulatory changes, and public scrutiny. Ethical leadership is not just about doing the right thing, it is about future-proofing an organization in an era where accountability is the expectation, not the exception.

Ethical Leadership in Practice

Ethical leadership is more than just an abstract ideal; it requires concrete, measurable actions. Leaders must go beyond symbolic gestures and implement policies that drive real change. Some of the most effective strategies include:

- Embedding ethics into corporate culture: Ensuring that ethical considerations are integrated into every aspect of decision-making, from hiring practices to supply chain management.

- Creating transparent reporting systems: Regularly publishing reports on sustainability initiatives, diversity efforts, and corporate social responsibility (CSR) commitments to maintain public accountability.

- Empowering employees to speak up: Encouraging open dialogue and whistleblower protection to ensure that unethical practices can be addressed without fear of retaliation.

- Holding leadership accountable: Ensuring that executives and managers are held to the same ethical standards as frontline employees, reinforcing a culture of integrity.

As the business landscape continues to evolve, ethical leadership will increasingly define which organizations thrive and which ones falter. The strongest leaders will be those who not only recognize their social and environmental responsibilities but actively embrace them as a core part of their leadership philosophy. The future belongs to those who lead with integrity, transparency, and a commitment to doing what is right—not just for their organizations, but for the world at large.

Adaptability in a Rapidly Changing Environment

The future is unpredictable, but great leaders are those who embrace uncertainty as an opportunity rather than a threat. Rapid technological advancements, economic shifts, and global crises demand leaders who are agile and prepared to pivot at a moment's notice. The organizations that survive and thrive in uncertain times are those led by individuals who are not bound by outdated models but instead cultivate a culture of continuous learning and innovation.

Lifelong learning is no longer a luxury but a necessity. Leaders must stay ahead of industry trends, proactively seek new knowledge, and foster environments where employees are encouraged to upskill and adapt. Those who fail to evolve risk becoming obsolete, as markets and consumer expectations shift faster than ever before.

Consider the organizations that have thrived in times of disruption. Companies like Netflix, which pivoted from DVD rentals to streaming before the industry caught on, and Tesla, which revolutionized the automotive industry by betting on electric vehicles when others hesitated, exemplify the power of adaptive leadership. These cases serve as reminders that future leaders must not only respond to change but anticipate and drive it.

Leadership in a Multigenerational Workforce

This is my absolute favorite topic because the younger generations are being unfairly criticized by older leaders and staff, not because they lack work ethic, but simply because they operate differently. They're not lazy; they just have a different approach to work, shaped by a rapidly evolving world.

For the first time in history, the workforce is composed of five generations working side by side: Baby Boomers, Generation X, Millennials, Generation Z, and now, the emerging Generation Alpha. Each generation brings distinct values, communication styles, and workplace expectations, making leadership more complex than ever.

The key to success lies in understanding and leveraging these differences rather than allowing them to create division.

Boomers and Gen Xers may prioritize stability, structure, and traditional hierarchies, while Millennials and Gen Z value flexibility, work-life balance, and purpose-driven careers. Meanwhile, Generation Alpha, the first fully digital-native generation, is poised to bring an entirely new approach to work, one that is deeply integrated with technology and innovation. Future leaders must develop strategies to bridge these generational gaps, fostering collaboration and mutual respect. Leadership approaches must be tailored to accommodate diverse needs—whether through mentorship programs that allow knowledge-sharing across generations or by implementing workplace policies that appeal to varying work styles.

A failure to recognize generational dynamics leads to disengagement and retention issues. But leaders who successfully integrate different perspectives create a richer, more innovative workforce that benefits from the wisdom of experience and the fresh thinking of emerging talent. It is particularly important to push back against the common misconception that younger generations, especially Gen Z and Gen Alpha, are lazy or entitled. The reality is that they are not less motivated; they are simply wired differently.

These younger generations grew up with technology as an extension of themselves. While older generations may see them as overly reliant on screens, they are, in fact, more adept at navigating digital landscapes, automating tasks, and leveraging artificial intelligence in ways that previous generations could never have imagined. Their ability to process information quickly, adapt to new tools, and collaborate in virtual spaces makes them a powerful asset to any organization. Leaders who embrace, support, and empower these younger generations will unlock a level of efficiency, creativity, and innovation that older generations may struggle to achieve alone.

Instead of resisting the changing workforce dynamics, forward-thinking leaders will tap into these strengths, integrating younger employees into leadership discussions, providing opportunities for reverse mentoring, and fostering an environment where the digital skills of Gen Z and Gen Alpha are fully utilized. The organizations that succeed in the future will not be those that demand younger employees conform to outdated work models, but those that recognize and harness their unique strengths. The future of leadership is not about dismissing the old or blindly accepting the new, it's about blending experience with innovation to create a workplace where every generation thrives.

The Shift Toward Purpose-Driven Leadership

The most effective leaders of the future will not be those who simply check boxes or execute corporate strategies without deeper meaning. Employees and consumers alike are drawn to organizations with a clear mission and impact-driven leadership. The shift toward purpose-driven leadership means that leaders must go beyond profitability and align their organizations with broader societal goals such as sustainability, social equity, and community well-being. But the key here is that leadership without purpose, a plan, and defined goals is meaningless. Without direction, a leader is just a person with a title on their hat— someone who holds authority but lacks the vision to make a difference.

True leadership is about action, not just position. A title alone does not inspire employees or drive success—purpose does. Leaders must develop a clear, strategic vision that aligns with both the organization's objectives and the evolving expectations of the workforce and consumers. Purpose-driven leaders set measurable goals, create roadmaps for execution, and ensure that every decision moves the organization forward in a meaningful way. Without a clear mission, leaders risk becoming stagnant, reactive, and ultimately ineffective in a world that demands agility and innovation.

This shift is already evident in industries across the board. Companies like Patagonia, which integrates environmental activism into its business model, and Microsoft, which has taken a firm stance on sustainability and social impact, showcase how purpose-driven leadership transforms industries. These organizations succeed not just because they have competent leaders, but because they have leaders with a defined mission; a reason beyond profits to push their teams forward.

Organizations that foster a culture of purpose attract and retain top talent, particularly among younger generations who prioritize meaning over monetary rewards. Employees want to work for leaders who have a vision, who communicate why their work matters, and who provide a roadmap for success. The leaders who will stand out in the future are those who understand that profitability and purpose are not mutually exclusive, but rather, deeply interconnected. When leaders establish a strong purpose, develop a clear plan, and set ambitious but achievable goals, they move from merely holding a title to actually leading with impact—and that is what sets great leaders apart.

Leadership in Action

The best way to understand the future of leadership is to examine organizations that have successfully navigated change, embraced disruption, and led with purpose. These case studies highlight how companies have leveraged adaptability, innovation, and social responsibility to redefine their industries. Here are several examples:

Netflix: Embracing Disruption

Netflix serves as one of the most compelling examples of adaptive leadership. Originally a DVD rental service was founded in 1997, the company disrupted the traditional video rental market dominated by Blockbuster. However, Netflix's real transformation began in the early 2000s when it foresaw the decline of physical media and the rise of digital streaming. Under the leadership of co-founder and former CEO Reed Hastings, the company shifted its business model, investing heavily in streaming technology despite initial financial risks.

This strategic pivot was not without challenges. The company had to negotiate licensing deals, build a reliable streaming infrastructure, and overcome skepticism from investors and consumers. However, by embracing change rather than resisting it, Netflix revolutionized entertainment consumption and became a global powerhouse. Today, it produces its own original content and competes with traditional Hollywood studios, demonstrating that future-ready leadership requires bold decision-making and the willingness to abandon outdated models in favor of emerging opportunities.

Tesla: Betting on the Future

Elon Musk's leadership at Tesla exemplifies the power of visionary thinking and calculated risk-taking. When Tesla launched in 2003, the automotive industry was deeply entrenched in gasoline-powered vehicles, and the idea of mainstream electric cars was widely dismissed as impractical. Yet, Musk saw the long-term potential of sustainable transportation and aggressively pushed for innovation despite industry skepticism.

Tesla's approach to leadership and disruption was twofold: technological advancement and market influence. The company did not just manufacture electric cars, it redefined the market by focusing on high-performance, desirable electric vehicles that could compete with luxury brands. Musk also made a controversial move by open-sourcing Tesla's patents, encouraging competition to drive EV adoption.

Tesla's success has forced legacy automakers to follow suit, with companies like Ford, GM, and Volkswagen now heavily investing in EVs. The case of Tesla underscores how leaders who embrace risk, challenge conventional wisdom, and persist despite resistance can fundamentally reshape entire industries.

Patagonia: Purpose Over Profit

Patagonia is a prime example of purpose-driven leadership that integrates social responsibility into its business model. Founded by Yvon Chouinard, Patagonia has consistently prioritized environmental sustainability over short-term profitability. The company has taken bold stances on climate change, sustainable manufacturing, and ethical labor practice actions that many corporations avoid for fear of alienating stakeholders.

One of Patagonia's most notable leadership decisions was its commitment to environmental activism. It has pledged 1% of its sales to environmental causes, developed sustainable supply chains, and even ran a controversial marketing campaign urging customers not to buy its products unless necessary to combat overconsumption. In 2022, Chouinard made an unprecedented move by transferring ownership of Patagonia to a trust dedicated to fighting climate change, ensuring that all future profits support environmental causes.

Unlike traditional corporations that focus solely on shareholder returns, Patagonia demonstrates that companies can be both financially successful and ethically responsible. The brand has cultivated an extremely loyal customer base and continues to thrive, proving that leadership rooted in purpose can drive both business success and global impact.

Unilever: Sustainability as a Business Strategy

Unilever, a multinational consumer goods company, has become a leader in corporate sustainability under the guidance of former CEO Paul Polman. Recognizing the growing demand for ethical business practices, Polman spearheaded the Unilever Sustainable Living Plan, a long-term strategy aimed at reducing the company's environmental footprint while improving social conditions worldwide.

This approach challenged traditional corporate thinking. Unilever took aggressive steps to reduce plastic waste, improve water efficiency, and create sustainable sourcing policies for raw materials. The company also emphasized fair labor practices and set ambitious goals to improve public health through its products.

Polman's leadership demonstrated that sustainability is not just an ethical obligation but a competitive advantage. Under his tenure, Unilever outperformed many of its industry rivals, proving that long-term sustainability strategies lead to stronger financial performance and brand trust. Today, Unilever remains a model for corporations looking to integrate sustainability into their core operations rather than treating it as an afterthought.

The success stories of Netflix, Tesla, Patagonia, and Unilever underscore a fundamental truth about leadership in the modern world—the future belongs to those who are willing to embrace change, take calculated risks, and lead with purpose. Each of these companies showcases a different facet of effective leadership: Netflix exemplifies the power of adaptability, proving that industries evolve rapidly and only those who anticipate and respond to change will thrive. Tesla demonstrates that visionary leadership, paired with relentless innovation, can disrupt even the most established industries. Patagonia serves as a model for purpose-driven leadership, showing that companies can balance profitability with ethical responsibility, while Unilever highlights how sustainability is not just a moral choice but a strategic business advantage.

What these examples collectively reveal is that leadership is no longer just about profitability, efficiency, or maintaining the status quo—it's about having a clear vision, taking decisive action, and aligning organizational goals with broader societal needs. The leaders who will shape the future will be those who embrace disruption rather than fear it, champion ethical responsibility rather than ignore it, and inspire rather than simply manage. Whether navigating technological advancements, shifting consumer expectations, or the complexities of a multigenerational workforce, the strongest leaders will be those who dare to challenge conventional wisdom and redefine success.

The takeaway for current and aspiring leaders is clear: leadership without purpose, innovation, and adaptability is merely a title. The organizations that will dominate the future will be those led by individuals who not only understand the demands of today but also have the foresight and courage to shape the world of tomorrow.

Leaders of Tomorrow Are Made Today

The future of leadership will be defined by adaptability, ethical responsibility, technological proficiency, and purpose-driven strategies. Leaders who fail to embrace change, leverage innovation, or prioritize transparency will find themselves obsolete in a world that no longer tolerates stagnation. The strongest organizations will not be led by those who cling to outdated models but by those who dare to challenge convention, take risks, and lead with conviction. Leadership is no longer about maintaining the status quo: it's about shaping the future.

As industries evolve, workforce demographics shift, and global challenges intensify, leadership must evolve with them. The next generation of leaders will not just manage organizations; they will inspire movements, drive progress, and redefine success. They will be bold enough to disrupt, wise enough to listen, and courageous enough to lead with purpose. They will understand that leadership is not about titles, power, or legacy: it's about impact, transformation, and leaving the world better than they found it.

The question is not whether leadership will change—it already has. The real question is: Who will rise to meet the challenge? The future belongs to those who do.

"The future of leadership belongs to those who embrace change, inspire trust, and balance innovation with humanity—leading not just with vision, but with integrity, adaptability, and a deep commitment to ethical progress"

Chapter 8

Leading with Purpose and Vision

Leadership is not just about holding a title, making decisions, or managing teams, it is about inspiring, guiding, and creating meaningful impact. Great leaders are not remembered for maintaining the status quo; they are remembered for their vision, integrity, and ability to transform organizations, industries, and even societies. As we conclude this exploration of leadership, we reflect on the essential principles that define true leadership and the ongoing journey of personal and professional growth.

Recap of Key Lessons

Throughout this book, we have examined the qualities and strategies that separate effective leaders from those who merely occupy a leadership role. At the core of successful leadership are vision, trust, adaptability, and resilience. These traits are not optional; they are essential for any leader who seeks to build a thriving organization and inspire those they lead.

Vision and Communication are the foundations of great leadership. Without a clear vision, leaders are simply reacting to circumstances rather than shaping the future. A strong vision provides direction, motivation, and purpose, ensuring that every decision aligns with a greater goal. However, vision is only effective if it is communicated clearly. Leaders must ensure that their teams understand not just the "what" but the "why" behind their work. Clarity in communication fosters alignment, engagement, and shared commitment to the organization's success.

Trust and Emotional Intelligence are equally critical. Leadership is not just about strategy; it is about people. Leaders who cultivate trust, empathy, and emotional intelligence create stronger, more engaged teams. Employees who trust their leaders are more committed, more productive, and more willing to innovate. The ability to listen, understand, and genuinely connect with others is just as important as making strategic decisions. A leader who lacks emotional intelligence may achieve short-term results but will struggle to build a sustainable, high-performing team.

Adaptability and Resilience have become non-negotiable traits in modern leadership. The world is evolving faster than ever—technology, market dynamics, and workforce expectations are shifting rapidly. Leaders who resist change, cling to old models, or refuse to adapt will find themselves left behind. True leadership requires resilience, the ability to navigate challenges, embrace uncertainty, and turn obstacles into opportunities rather than roadblocks. The best leaders are those who learn from setbacks, pivot when necessary, and lead their teams through uncertainty with confidence.

These fundamental principles form the foundation of great leadership, but the work of becoming a great leader never stops. Leadership is an ongoing practice—it requires continuous growth, self-reflection, and a commitment to lifelong learning. The best leaders never stop evolving because they understand that great leadership is not about reaching a final destination—it is about continuously striving to inspire, innovate, and improve.

The Evolving Role of Leadership

Leadership has undergone a profound transformation over time. Gone are the days when it was solely about authority, hierarchy, and rigid control. In the past, leadership was often defined by a top-down approach—leaders gave orders, employees followed, and organizations operated within strictly defined structures. While this model may have worked in a world of predictability and stability, it is no longer viable in today's fast-paced, interconnected, and ever-changing global landscape.

Modern leadership is dynamic. It requires flexibility, collaboration, and emotional intelligence to inspire and engage employees. Today's leaders must navigate complexity, embrace inclusivity, and make decisions in an increasingly transparent world. The rise of remote work, digital transformation, and diverse workforce demographics means that leadership must go beyond merely giving instructions—it must be about building trust, fostering innovation, and empowering teams to thrive in an environment of constant change.

The challenges of leadership are also greater than ever before. Leaders today must contend with technological advancements that disrupt entire industries, generational shifts in the workforce, and global crises such as climate change, social inequality, and economic uncertainty. Employees and consumers alike demand more from leaders—they expect authenticity, accountability, and a commitment to social and environmental responsibility. A failure to adapt to these realities will not only weaken a leader's effectiveness but also erode trust and relevance in an increasingly value-driven society.

A solid leader understands that evolution is key to continued success and that stagnation is a slow death—a path that leads to irrelevance, disengagement, and ultimately, failure. Organizations that fail to evolve do not just fall behind, they collapse. The business world is littered with examples of once-great companies that refused to innovate and paid the price with their own extinction. Leaders who cling to outdated models of power and control will find themselves leading teams that resist, businesses that shrink, and a future that leaves them behind.

To remain relevant, leaders must continuously evolve. The best leaders never stop learning, seeking feedback, and refining their approach. Leadership is not about having all the answers, it is about asking the right questions, fostering curiosity, and staying adaptable in the face of uncertainty. The leaders of tomorrow will not be those who cling to old habits, but those who embrace change, encourage collaboration, and lead with integrity.

Ultimately, leadership is not about holding a position, it is about making an impact. The future belongs to those who see change not as a threat, but as an opportunity to innovate, inspire, and create lasting value. The question is not whether leadership will evolve—it already has. The real question is: Are you ready to evolve with it, or will you be left behind?

Embracing a Growth Mindset

A fixed mindset sees failure as a dead end, an indication of unchangeable limitations. A growth mindset, on the other hand, sees failure as a steppingstone, an opportunity to learn, improve, and evolve. Great leaders do not fear challenges, they embrace them. They understand that setbacks are not proof of incompetence but rather a natural part of progress. In a rapidly changing world, the ability to learn, adapt, and grow is more valuable than simply maintaining the status quo.

Encouraging a growth mindset within an organization fosters a culture of curiosity, innovation, and resilience. Employees who feel safe to experiment, take calculated risks, and learn from mistakes are more likely to bring fresh ideas, push boundaries, and continuously improve. Leaders who create an environment where learning is encouraged, rather than punished—unlock the full potential of their teams. When employees fear failure, they play it safe, avoid risks, and resist change, ultimately stifling creativity and progress. Leaders who embrace a culture of learning create organizations that thrive, even in the face of uncertainty.

To cultivate a growth mindset within an organization, leaders can take several actionable steps:

- Encourage continuous learning: Invest in professional development, mentorship programs, and cross-functional training. When employees are given opportunities to learn new skills and broaden their expertise, they become more engaged, capable, and prepared for the future. Leaders should provide resources, time, and incentives for employees to develop both personally and professionally.

- Reward innovation: Recognize and celebrate new ideas, even when they do not immediately succeed. Not every innovation will be an instant breakthrough, but fostering a culture where employees feel encouraged to experiment ensures that progress is always being made. Failure should be seen as a learning opportunity rather than a career setback.

- Lead by example: Demonstrate your own willingness to adapt, learn, and improve rather than pretending to have all the answers. Leaders who show humility and a commitment to growth inspire their teams to do the same. Instead of expecting perfection, they encourage problem-solving, iteration, and continuous development.

When leaders model a growth mindset, they inspire their teams to embrace challenges with confidence rather than fear. This mindset is what separates stagnant organizations from those that continuously evolve and thrive in an ever-changing world. The most successful leaders and companies are not those who avoid failure, but those who learn, adapt, and come back stronger every time.

Ensuring Continued Success

True leadership is not about personal accolades or individual success, it is about ensuring the continued success of an organization long after a leader's tenure has ended. The best leaders do not focus on making a name for themselves; they focus on developing other leaders and strengthening the systems, values, and culture that will sustain the organization for generations to come. Leadership should never be a one-person show, it should be a shared effort that empowers others to rise, take ownership, and contribute to long-term growth.

A strong leadership pipeline ensures that an organization is not dependent on a single individual but is instead built on a foundation of mentorship, collaboration, and strategic development. Without intentional leadership cultivation, companies become vulnerable to stagnation, instability, and succession crises. Great organizations are not built on the strength of one leader alone; they thrive when leadership is distributed, nurtured, and continuously evolving.

The best leaders invest in people because they know that an organization's greatest asset is its talent. They actively mentor, coach, and empower others to take on leadership roles, ensuring that future generations of leaders are prepared to carry the mission forward. This strengthens the organization, fuels innovation, and creates a workplace where employees feel valued, motivated, and inspired to contribute. A company that relies too heavily on one or two key figures is doomed to falter the moment those individuals step away. The true test of leadership is not how well an organization runs under a single leader but how well it continues to succeed once that leader is gone.

Key Actions to Build a Lasting Leadership Structure:

- Mentor future leaders: Great leaders don't just lead—they develop others to lead as well. Sharing knowledge, providing guidance, and creating opportunities for others to step up ensures that leadership is a continuous cycle, not a singular event.

- Foster a culture of leadership at all levels: Leadership is not just for executives. Encourage leadership qualities in employees, regardless of their title or tenure. When leadership is integrated into every level of the organization, teams become more proactive, engaged, and invested in collective success.

- Prioritize succession planning: Leadership development should not be an afterthought. Organizations must have a clear plan for leadership transitions, ensuring that knowledge, strategy, and vision are carried forward seamlessly.

A great leader's impact is not measured by what they built alone but by who they empowered to build even more. The strongest organizations do not crumble when a leader departs; they flourish because the leadership structure has been intentionally designed to endure. The leaders of today must not only focus on achieving current success but on ensuring that their organizations will thrive long into the future.

Leadership as a Force for Good

Leadership extends beyond the workplace. The most impactful leaders understand that their influence carries weight far beyond corporate boardrooms and balance sheets—they recognize their broader responsibility to society and use their position to drive meaningful changes in social, environmental, and ethical matters. The true measure of leadership is not just profitability but impact—the ability to make a lasting difference in the world.

In today's world, leadership is no longer just about profits and performance metrics. Employees, customers, and stakeholders expect organizations to stand for something greater. The rise of conscious capitalism has redefined business success—leaders who prioritize ethical decision-making, sustainability, diversity, and corporate responsibility are not only doing the right thing, but they are also building stronger, more resilient organizations. Companies that ignore these expectations risk losing talent, alienating customers, and falling behind in an increasingly value-driven marketplace.

Leaders who embrace their role as a force for good do more than make statements; they take action. They lead initiatives that address climate change, economic inequality, and workplace inclusivity. They invest in social programs, advocate for fair labor practices, and push for sustainable business models that benefit both people and the planet. This is not about philanthropy alone, it's about embedding purpose into the very core of how businesses operate.

Examples of Purpose-Driven Leadership

Some of the most respected and successful leaders in the world have demonstrated that businesses can thrive while making a positive impact:

- Yvon Chouinard (Patagonia): Built a company that prioritizes environmental sustainability over short-term profits. Patagonia has donated millions to conservation efforts, implemented sustainable supply chains, and even transferred company ownership to a trust dedicated to fighting climate change, ensuring that profits serve a greater mission.

- Paul Polman (Unilever): Led a global shift toward long-term sustainability while maintaining financial success. Under his leadership, Unilever committed to reducing carbon emissions, eliminating plastic waste, and improving fair trade practices, proving that corporations can be both profitable and responsible.

- Reed Hastings (Netflix): Transformed the entertainment industry through innovation while championing workplace culture and inclusion. Netflix has been at the forefront of progressive workplace policies, diversity initiatives, and creative freedom, setting a new standard for corporate responsibility in the media sector.

These leaders understood that success is not just measured in revenue but in the lasting impact they leave on their industries and the world. Their leadership extended beyond the boardroom—they inspired movements, influenced policies, and set new standards for responsible business practices.

True Leadership is About Purpose, Not Just Power

True leadership is not about holding power or increasing shareholder returns, it is about using influence for the greater good. Leaders who define the future will be those who align their organizations with missions that benefit both people and the planet.

The best leaders inspire others to think beyond immediate gains and to consider long-term impact. They create workplaces where employees feel proud of their contributions, where customers feel connected to a greater cause, and where stakeholders see value beyond profit margins.

In the end, the question every leader should ask themselves is not just "How much did my organization earn?" but "How much did my leadership matter?" The strongest leaders will be remembered not only for what they built but for the positive change they sparked, the people they empowered, and the world they helped shape.

Lead with Intent

Leadership is a responsibility, not just a position. It is not about the authority granted by a title, but about the impact you make, the trust you build, and the legacy you leave behind. The lessons shared in this book are not just theories or abstract concepts, they are a call to action. The world needs leaders who act with purpose, lead with integrity, and inspire those around them to be better.

To those who are already in leadership roles: Step up. Take responsibility, and lead with intent. Do not lead just for the sake of holding a title—lead because you have a vision worth pursuing. Leadership is about service, influence, and making a difference in the lives of the people you guide. Your title does not define you, your actions do. Be the leader who inspires, who builds trust, who drives innovation, and who creates an environment where people can thrive. The greatest leaders are those who lift others up, who empower teams, and who ensure that success continues long after they are gone.

To aspiring leaders: Do not wait for permission. Leadership is not confined to a title or a position at the top of an organizational chart. It is about initiative, influence, and integrity. Leadership can begin anywhere—in your workplace, your community, or even within your family. If you wait for someone to grant you the authority to lead, you may never take that first step. Instead, own your growth, seek knowledge, and lead where you are. Every great leader started somewhere, and those who make the biggest impact are the ones who take initiative and embrace challenges rather than waiting for opportunities to come to them.

The world does not need more managers, it needs leaders with vision, courage, and purpose. It needs people who are willing to make tough decisions, challenge the status quo, and push forward despite uncertainty. Leadership is about creating positive change, in your organization, in your community, and in the world. The question is not whether you can lead—the question is whether you will.

Finally, leadership is not a destination, it is a journey. There is no final stage where a leader can say, "I have arrived." The best leaders never stop growing, never stop learning, and never stop striving to make a difference. Leadership is not about achieving a certain title or reaching a particular milestone—it is about continuous self-improvement, the pursuit of excellence, and the unwavering commitment to lead with purpose.

There will always be obstacles, resistance, and setbacks. There will be moments of doubt and times when leadership feels overwhelming. But true leaders push forward despite them. They recognize that failure is not the end but an opportunity to learn and grow. They understand that leadership is not about having all the answers, it is about asking the right questions, listening intently, and making decisions with courage and conviction.

Leadership is not for the faint of heart. It requires strength, resilience, and the ability to inspire others even in difficult times. But for those who embrace the challenge, leadership is one of the most rewarding and transformative journeys a person can take. It is a path that allows you to influence lives, drive progress, and create a legacy of impact that extends beyond yourself.

As you move forward, remember this: The world is shaped by those who choose to lead. Every great movement, every breakthrough innovation, and every societal change has been driven by people who had the courage to step up, take risks, and lead with conviction. The future will be defined by those who dare to lead—those who see challenges as opportunities, who lift others up, and who refuse to settle for mediocrity.

The question is not whether leadership will evolve—it already has. The real question is: Will you rise to meet the challenge? Will you choose to lead?

"Leadership is not about maintaining the status quo; it's about embracing change, inspiring growth, and creating a vision that motivates others to reach beyond what seems possible—transforming challenges into opportunities and ideas into lasting impact"

Chapter 9

Navigating the Leadership Minefield

Being a Leader is not just about making the right decision; it is about avoiding the wrong ones. Many leaders begin their journey with good intentions, yet some find themselves entangled in the minefield of leadership pitfalls, ego-driven decisions, toxic behaviors, misplaced ambition, and an over-reliance on fear. These missteps do not just damage a leader's reputation; they can cripple an organization, alienate teams, and erode trust beyond repair.

One of the most telling signs of poor-quality leadership is the promotion of unhealthy competition within a team. These leaders create an environment where employees are pitted against one another, not to drive better results, but to belittle those around them and elevate their own sense of superiority. This kind of behavior breeds resentment, lowers morale, and shifts the focus from collective success to individual survival. Such leaders are quick to point out faults in others, but rarely take accountability for their own shortcomings, further eroding the trust and unity needed for organizational success.

In contrast, a great leader is easy to identify, they work for the betterment of the organization, not their ego. They focus on collaboration, fostering a culture where every team member feels valued and supported. These leaders actively promote junior employees, mentoring them to develop their skills and preparing them for future leadership roles. By building others up, they create a legacy of strong, capable leaders who are equipped to carry the organization forward.

Understanding the dangers of poor leadership is just as important as understanding what makes a great leader. The following sections expose some of the most dangerous leadership traps, offering insights into how they manifest, their consequences, and how to avoid them. Great leadership isn't just about personal success; it's about ensuring the success of the organization and those who will lead it in the future.

The Pitfalls of Ego-Driven Leadership

Some leaders step into their roles not to serve, but to be seen. They are more concerned with personal recognition than with team success, treating leadership as a platform for self-promotion rather than a responsibility to guide, support, and uplift those they lead. Instead of empowering their teams, they seek to dominate and control, ensuring that every success is attributed to them while failures are deflected onto others. Collaboration takes a backseat to their need for authority, and decision-making becomes less about what's best for the organization and more about maintaining their own image.

Ego-driven leadership often manifests in several damaging ways. These leaders take credit for team achievements while conveniently placing the blame on others when things go wrong. Rather than recognizing and appreciating the contributions of their employees, they act as though every success was the result of their own genius. They also refuse to listen to feedback, believing that their perspective is the only one that matters. Instead of fostering a culture of continuous learning and improvement, they dismiss input from others, shutting down ideas that do not align with their own. Additionally, they tend to micromanage and override decisions, ensuring that only their ideas move forward. This behavior not only slows down progress but also erodes trust and confidence within the team, employees begin to feel that their expertise is undervalued, their voices unheard, and their contributions insignificant.

Ego-driven leadership is not just toxicity, it is destructive and counterproductive. When a leader is more concerned with their own status, recognition, or personal agenda than with the growth and well-being of the team, they alienate their employees, stifle innovation, and foster resentment. A workplace dominated by ego discourages creativity, risk-taking, and independent problem-solving because employees become more focused on avoiding criticism than on contributing ideas. Over time, talented employees lose motivation and disengage, choosing either to mentally check out or leave the organization altogether.

An organization suffering under ego-driven leadership does not thrive, it struggles. Instead of progress, there is stagnation. Instead of collaboration, there is competition for approval. Instead of trust, there is fear. The best leaders understand that leadership is not about elevating oneself, it is about elevating others. Those who lead with humility, self-awareness, and a genuine desire to serve their teams build organizations where people feel valued, motivated, and empowered to do their best work.

Real-World Consequences of Ego-Driven Leadership

Consider the downfall of once-prominent companies where leaders allowed ego to override sound judgment. Time and time again, history has shown that when leaders prioritize their own pride over reality, organizations suffer. CEOs who ignore warnings signs from their teams, refused to adapt to industry changes, or made reckless decisions solely to prove their own brilliance have driven multi-billion-dollar enterprises into the ground. Rather than listening to the experts around them, they insisted on their own way, dismissing concerns and overlooking critical market shifts.

From failed product launches to catastrophic financial mismanagement, the corporate graveyard is filled with cautionary tales of leaders who let their arrogance blind them to reality. Blockbuster refused to embrace streaming, believing that its physical rental model was too big to fail—until Netflix made it obsolete. Kodak, once a dominant force in photography, dismissed the shift to digital cameras, leading to its eventual collapse. These failures were not due to a lack of resources or opportunities, but rather a failure in leadership, specifically, an unwillingness to adapt, listen, and evolve.

Great leadership requires humility. The most effective leaders understand that success is a team effort, not an individual achievement. They encourage input from those around them, regardless of rank, knowing that the best ideas often come from those closest to work. Most importantly, they are willing to admit mistakes, adjust course, and place the organization's success over their personal ego. These leaders do not view themselves as the smartest person in the room, they surround themselves with talented people and listen. They recognize that their role is to guide, not to dictate.

In leadership, ego is not a strength—it is a liability. Leaders who fail to recognize their own limitations, dismiss feedback, and place their reputation over results are destined to make decisions that ultimately harm the very organizations they claim to lead. True strength in leadership comes from humility, self-awareness, and a willingness to grow—not from insisting on always being right.

The Toxic Leader Syndrome

A toxic leader is not just a bad boss, they are a corrosive force that slowly erodes the foundation of an organization. Toxic leadership is not just about poor management; it is destructive, manipulative, and deeply rooted in insecurity. These leaders do not simply make mistakes, they create an environment where morale is low, turnover is high, and dysfunction becomes the norm. Employees under toxic leadership often feel undervalued, powerless, and mentally exhausted, leading to decreased productivity and a culture where fear and resentment replace motivation and innovation.

Signs of Toxic Leadership

One of the most dangerous aspects of toxic leadership is that it can be subtle at first. Many toxic leaders present themselves as assertive, confident, or ambitious, but over time, their behaviors chip away at trust, create division, and stifle team success. Some of the most common red flags of toxic leadership include:

- Manipulation: Toxic leaders use gaslighting, deception, or guilt to maintain control over employees. They twist situations to make employees doubt their own judgment, creating an environment where individuals second-guess themselves and fear speaking up. Instead of offering guidance and support, they intentionally create confusion to retain power, ensuring that their team remains dependent on their leadership rather than empowered to think independently.

- Favoritism: Rather than rewarding hard work and talent, toxic leaders prioritize loyalty over competence. They promote and give opportunities to those who flatter them, agree with them, or enable their behavior, rather than to those who actually deserve it based on merit. This creates an environment of resentment and disengagement, where truly skilled employees become discouraged, knowing that success is based on who you know rather than what you contribute. Over time, this destroys morale and weakens the overall performance of the organization.

- Creating a Hostile Work Environment: Toxic leaders thrive on control, and one of their most effective tactics is creating fear-based cultures. They may publicly humiliate employees, use intimidation tactics, or foster a cutthroat, hyper-competitive work environment where colleagues are pitted against one another instead of working together. This leads to high stress, anxiety, and burnout, making employees dread coming to work and causing top talent to leave at the first opportunity.

Toxic leadership is a poison that spreads, the longer it is left unchecked, the more damage it does. Organizations that allow toxic leaders to remain in power will see high turnover, declining performance, and an overall loss of trust in leadership. The best leaders do not manipulate or intimidate, they inspire, support, and build up their teams. Leadership is not about domination—it is about empowerment. Those who lead through fear, favoritism, and manipulation may hold power for a while, but ultimately, their organizations will suffer the consequences of their toxicity.

The Long-Term Damage of Toxic Leadership

Toxic leadership is like a slow poison that seeps into every corner of an organization, weakening its foundation and crippling its ability to grow and succeed. The damage it inflicts is often not immediate, making it even more dangerous. Leaders may not recognize the problem until it has already driven away top talent, shattered morale, and embedded dysfunction into the company's culture. Employees subjected to toxic leadership often feel unappreciated and undervalued, leading to disengagement, low motivation, and a gradual loss of passion for their work. When employees believe that their hard work goes unnoticed while manipulative or incompetent colleagues are rewarded, they disengage, doing only the bare minimum required to keep their jobs.

Beyond just disengagement, toxic leadership creates a culture where innovation and risk-taking are punished. In such environments, employees become afraid to speak up, challenge ideas, or bring forward creative solutions because they worry about retaliation, humiliation, or being dismissed outright. This kills innovation and problem-solving, as employees learn that compliance is valued over critical thinking. Over time, this fosters a workplace where stagnation replaces growth, and fear stifles ambition.

Perhaps the most destructive consequence of toxic leadership is the constant stress, burnout, and high turnover it generates. When employees are forced to work under leaders who micromanage, belittle, or manipulate, stress levels skyrocket. A once-excited, dedicated workforce turns into a tired, anxious, and emotionally drained team that is simply trying to survive. High-performing employees, those who know their worth, will be the first to leave, unwilling to tolerate an environment where leadership is toxic and abusive. What remains are the disengaged, the fearful, and those who lack the confidence to walk away, further deepening the cycle of dysfunction.

The best organizations do not tolerate toxic leadership. They take proactive measures to identify and remove toxic leaders before they poison the entire culture. Companies that turn a blind eye to toxic leadership may experience short-term results, but in the long run, they will suffer irreversible damage—losing talent, credibility, and the trust of their workforce. True leadership is not about control, fear, or manipulation, it is about empowering others, fostering trust, and leading with integrity. Organizations that recognize this distinction will thrive, while those that ignore it will eventually collapse under the weight of their own dysfunction.

Leaders Who Run at the Chance to Be a Leader (Bad Leader)

Not everyone who steps into leadership does so for the right reasons. While leadership should be a responsibility driven by purpose, service, and a commitment to making a difference, some pursue leadership purely for status, power, and personal gain. Others, in contrast, accept leadership reluctantly—not because they seek recognition, but because they feel a deep sense of duty to step up when needed.

The difference between these two types of leaders is profound. One leads because they crave authority; the other leads because they understand the weight of responsibility. One demands respect; the other earns it. One focuses on self-promotion, the other on team success. Organizations that fail to distinguish between these two types of leaders' risk promoting individuals who may ultimately harm the organization rather than help it grow.

The Power-Hungry Wannabe (Bad Leader)

Some individuals actively seek out leadership positions, not because they want to serve, mentor, or improve the organization, but because they crave status, control, and authority. These "leaderless leaders" run for leadership roles not to inspire and uplift others but to elevate themselves. Their leadership is built on self-interest, and their motivation stems from ego rather than genuine commitment.

This type of leader often:

- Campaigns for leadership roles without a clear vision. They focus more on winning the position rather than understanding what it actually takes to lead. Their primary goal is to secure authority, not to develop meaningful strategies or make a lasting impact.

- Desires leadership for the perks, prestige, or influence it grants them. These individuals see leadership as a reward, not a responsibility. They want the title, the recognition, and the perceived power, but they lack the self-awareness and humility necessary to lead effectively.

- Struggles to lead effectively because they lack genuine leadership skills or passion. Without a real commitment to leadership principles, they fail to inspire their teams, make informed decisions, or create a culture of trust and accountability.

Leaders who chase titles rather than embrace responsibility ultimately fail their teams and their organizations. Instead of inspiring loyalty and respect, they create resentment and disengagement. Their need to assert authority, micromanage, and make everything about themselves leads to poor decision-making, lack of innovation, and a toxic work environment. They may achieve temporary success, but their inability to genuinely lead will ultimately cause more harm than good.

A true leader does not pursue leadership for self-serving reasons. They step into the role because they see a need and rise to meet it. They understand that leadership is not about being in the spotlight, it is about shining a light on others. Organizations must learn to differentiate between those who chase power and those who embrace responsibility because placing the wrong person in a leadership role can have devastating consequences.

Leader Accepts Out of Duty (Good Leader)

On the other side of the leadership spectrum are the reluctant leaders, those who do not seek out leadership for the sake of power, prestige, or personal advancement, but who step up out of a deep sense of responsibility. These individuals often never intended to lead, but when faced with a situation where leadership is needed, they rise to the occasion. They take on leadership not for the title, but because they recognize that their skills, experience, and commitment can make a meaningful difference.

Unlike power-hungry leaders who chase authority, these reluctant leaders:

- Accept leadership roles because they genuinely believe they can contribute and improve the organization. They do not view leadership as a personal victory but as a responsibility to guide and support others.

- Lead with humility and a sense of duty rather than self-promotion. Instead of demanding recognition, they focus on doing the right thing, often working behind the scenes to ensure the team's success.

- Empower others and prioritize team success over personal gain. They see leadership not as a means of control, but as a way to bring out the best in others.

These are the leaders who earn respect naturally, who foster collaboration and create real, lasting change. They do not chase leadership, they become leaders because their team trusts them to lead.

They listen more than they speak, they encourage rather than dictate, and they recognize that a leader's job is to serve, not to be served.

Organizations that identify and cultivate reluctant leaders will always have strong, principled leadership at their core. These individuals may not seek the spotlight, but they are the ones who drive real progress, leading not through force or ego, but through dedication, integrity, and a genuine commitment to those they serve.

Leadership by Fear vs. Leadership by Respect

A leader can command authority in two ways, by instilling fear or by earning respect. The difference is profound, and the impact on an organization is transformative. Fear-driven leadership may produce short-term compliance, but respect-driven leadership builds long-term success.

The Consequences of Fear-Based Leadership

Leaders who rule by fear believe that strict control, intimidation, and punishment are the best ways to maintain order and drive performance. However, fear-based leadership is unsustainable and creates a toxic work environment that discourages engagement, innovation, and long-term commitment.

Fear-driven leaders often:

- Micromanage and intimidate rather than trust and empower. Employees under fear-based leaders feel constantly scrutinized and never truly trusted to do their jobs. This results in low confidence, high stress, and reduced initiative.

- Suppress creativity because employees are too afraid to take risks. When workers are punished for mistakes or ideas that don't work out, they stop thinking outside the box, and the organization becomes stagnant. Innovation requires a safe space for trial and error, fear eliminates that space.

- Drive high turnover rates as employees leave to escape a toxic work environment. People do not stay where they feel unvalued or emotionally exhausted. High turnover is expensive and disruptive, and companies that cultivate fear-based leadership eventually find themselves hemorrhaging talent and struggling to attract top performers.

Fear-based leadership might yield short-term compliance, but in the long run, it cripples innovation, destroys morale, and leads to organizational decline. Employees perform at the bare minimum—not out of passion, but out of fear of punishment. Eventually, fear erodes trust, weakens teamwork, and fosters resentment that can cripple even the most powerful organizations.

The Power of Respect-Driven Leadership

In contrast, leaders who earn respect rather than demand obedience create workplaces where employees feel valued, motivated, and inspired to contribute. Respect-driven leadership is not about authority, it is about influence. People do not follow these leaders because they are forced to, they follow them because they believe in them.

Leaders who build respect-based workplaces:

- Foster loyalty, commitment, and long-term employee engagement. Employees who feel respected and supported are more invested in the company's success and are far more likely to go the extra mile.

- Encourage open dialogue, where employees feel heard and valued. Unlike fear-driven leaders who shut down conversation, respect-driven leaders welcome feedback, input, and differing perspectives, recognizing that true strength lies in diversity of thought.

- Create a culture of innovation, where ideas are welcomed rather than silenced. People thrive in environments where they feel safe to think creatively, experiment, and propose new ideas. When

134

employees know their contributions are valued rather than punished, they are far more likely to drive meaningful innovation.

Fear vs. Respect: A Case Study in Leadership Outcomes

Consider the difference between two types of leaders in a struggling company:

- Leader A sees declining profits and immediately begins firing employees, increasing demands, and implementing rigid micromanagement. The workforce shrinks under stress, and employees begin leaving, not because of performance issues, but to escape the toxic culture. The company spirals downward, caught in a cycle of blame, disengagement, and stagnation.

- Leader B sees the same challenge but takes a different approach. Instead of resorting to punitive measures, they engage the team, invite collaboration, and seek input on solutions. Employees feel valued and trusted, morale improves, and the team works together to drive innovation and turn the company around.

The outcome? Leader A creates a company that collapses under fear. Leader B builds a company that thrives through respect and resilience.

Choosing the Right Leadership Path

Leadership is not just about authority—it's about impact. The true test of leadership is not how much fear a leader can command, but how much trust and respect they can earn.

Fear-based leaders may hold power, but they never truly inspire. Their employees work out of obligation, not dedication. They may see short-term compliance, but they never see lasting success.

Respect-driven leaders, however, build something far greater, a workplace where people want to be, where employees give their best effort because they believe in the mission, the vision, and the leadership itself. These are the leaders who transform organizations, empower individuals, and leave a legacy of growth and success.

The choice is clear: Will you lead through fear and control, or will you build an organization where people thrive through trust and respect?

Case Study: Fear vs. Respect in Action

Consider two leaders facing the same organizational crisis: a company experiencing declining profits, market instability, and a demoralized workforce. The way these two leaders respond to the challenge determines the fate of the company and its employees.

Leader A: Leading Through Fear

Leader A sees the numbers slipping and panics. They immediately implement harsh cost-cutting measures, including layoffs, increased workloads, and rigid performance controls. Employees, already stressed by the financial downturn, are now living in fear, unsure if they will be the next to lose their jobs. Instead of engaging the workforce in solutions, Leader A tightens control, monitoring employees excessively, limiting flexibility, and demanding immediate results without providing a clear path forward.

The impact is devastating. Employees feel disposable, leading to resentment, disengagement, and an exodus of top talent. Creativity plummets because employees are too afraid to take risks or propose new ideas—they know failure will be punished, not treated as a learning opportunity. The company, now operating in survival mode, loses its innovative edge, struggles to maintain productivity, and eventually collapses under the weight of poor morale, high turnover, and a toxic work culture.

Leader B: Leading Through Respect

Leader B faces the same crisis but chooses a different path. Instead of resorting to immediate, fear-based reactions, they take a step back and analyze the situation with their team. They hold open discussions with employees, explaining the company's challenges while inviting ideas, feedback, and solutions. Rather than demanding compliance, Leader B motivates the workforce through transparency and shared goals, creating a collective sense of purpose rather than a culture of fear.

Employees feel valued and invested in turning the company around. Knowing their ideas matter, they proactively contribute solutions, innovate, and take ownership of their roles. Instead of fleeing a sinking ship, employees work harder to reinvent the company, improving processes, cutting inefficiencies, and developing new strategies that drive the business forward.

The outcome? Leader A creates a company that collapses under fear. Leader B builds a company that transforms setbacks into growth, fostering resilience, innovation, and long-term success.

This case study highlights a critical truth: how a leader reacts to adversity determines the trajectory of an organization. Fear breeds stagnation and collapse. Respect fosters loyalty, engagement, and long-term resilience.

What is the Right Leadership Path

Leadership is full of challenges, crises, and high-stakes decisions, but the greatest test of a leader is how they handle power. Some wield power to control, intimidate, and dominate, while others use it to empower, uplift, and build trust. The difference between self-serving leaders and great leaders is not just in their methods, but in their motives.

The best leaders do not lead for personal ambition or ego—they lead to serve, to elevate others, and to create a culture of trust, collaboration, and success. They do not see leadership as a status symbol but as a responsibility to be carried with integrity and vision.

Great leaders:

- Prioritize the team over personal ambition – They understand that success is never about the individual at the top, but about the collective strength of the organization. They create environments where everyone thrives, not just themselves.

- Remove toxicity and foster trust – They proactively address toxic behaviors, ensuring that manipulation, fear, and favoritism have no place in the organization. They create workplaces where employees feel safe, heard, and respected.

- Embrace leadership as a responsibility, not a privilege – Leadership is not about power; it is about service. The most effective leaders understand that their role is to support, guide, and nurture those they lead.

The true mark of leadership is not how much fear a leader commands, but how much respect they earn. Employees may comply with fear-driven leadership, but they will never be truly invested, engaged, or loyal. Respect-driven leadership inspires lasting success, built on trust, collaboration, and a shared vision.

The Choice is Yours

Every leader faces a choice, will you lead through fear and control, creating a culture of compliance, stagnation, and inevitable decline? Or will you lead with integrity, vision, and respect, building a team that is inspired, innovative, and driven to achieve greatness?

Leadership is not just about holding a position, it is about the impact you create and the legacy you leave behind. Choose wisely.

"Leadership isn't about holding power—it's about building trust, fostering collaboration, and avoiding the minefields of ego and toxicity that cripple teams and destroy progress. The strongest leaders inspire through humility, not fear, and elevate others to achieve greatness together"

Chapter 10

Breaking the Cycle of Failed Leadership

Perfection is not always the goal of leadership, it is about growth, accountability, and continuous improvement. Many organizations suffer from repetitive cycles of failed leadership, where poor leadership habits are passed down, normalized, or ignored until they become deeply ingrained in the company culture. This cycle leads to low morale, high turnover, disengaged employees, and stagnation. However, it is possible to break free from the pattern of ineffective leadership by fostering self-awareness, embracing feedback, rebuilding trust after missteps, and cultivating a culture that prioritizes strong leadership values.

Breaking the cycle of failed leadership is not just about removing bad leaders, it is about redefining leadership itself within an organization. It requires commitment at every level to identify, develop, and empower leaders who can inspire, engage, and build organizations where people thrive.

The Role of Self-Awareness in Leadership Growth

Leadership failure often begins with a lack of self-awareness. Leaders who fail to recognize their own weaknesses, blind spots, and limitations are more likely to make poor decisions, ignore feedback, and alienate their teams. Without self-awareness, a leader can become disconnected from the realities of their organization, failing to see how their actions affect morale, engagement, and productivity. A leader who cannot objectively assess their own effectiveness is likely to create unnecessary obstacles for their team, leading to frustration, stagnation, and ultimately, failure.

True leadership growth starts with deep, honest reflection. This requires a willingness to assess one's strengths and shortcomings, to ask hard questions about leadership effectiveness, and to be open to constructive criticism. Leaders must be willing to examine not just their successes but also their failures, and use those insights to adapt, improve, and grow.

A strong leader must continuously ask themselves:

- Am I listening more than I speak?

  Leadership is not about having all the answers, it is about asking the right questions and truly hearing the perspectives of others. Leaders who dominate conversations and refuse to listen to feedback create a culture where employees feel unheard and undervalued.

- Do I seek out and genuinely consider feedback from my team?

  A leader who actively seeks constructive input fosters a culture of trust and continuous improvement. Employees respect leaders who are willing to listen, learn, and adjust their approach based on feedback.

- Am I aware of how my actions affect morale, engagement, and productivity?

  Leaders set the tone and culture of an organization. A leader's behavior, whether positive or negative, has a ripple effect on employee motivation, collaboration, and overall workplace satisfaction.

- Am I leading with integrity, empathy, and a vision for the future?

  The most effective leaders are those who lead with purpose and authenticity, balancing strategic decision-making with genuine care for their team. They do not just manage people; they inspire, guide, and support them toward a shared vision.

Self-awareness is not a one-time realization—it is an ongoing process. The best leaders continually assess, adjust, and evolve, understanding that growth and development never stop. Those who cultivate self-awareness become stronger, more adaptable, and more impactful leaders, while those who resist it risk falling into patterns of poor leadership that harm both their teams and their organizations.

Tools and Strategies for Cultivating Self-Awareness

Becoming a self-aware leader does not happen by accident—it requires intentional effort, consistent reflection, and a willingness to receive and act on feedback. Leaders who prioritize self-awareness are better equipped to understand their impact, make informed decisions, and create a positive work environment. They recognize that leadership is not about always having the right answers but about asking the right questions and striving for constant improvement.

There are several effective strategies leaders can use to cultivate self-awareness:

- 360-Degree Feedback: One of the most valuable ways to gain insight into leadership effectiveness is through 360-degree feedback. This process involves gathering input from peers, subordinates, and supervisors to develop a comprehensive, unbiased perspective on one's leadership strengths and areas for improvement. While it can be uncomfortable to hear constructive criticism, leaders who embrace this feedback can identify blind spots and make meaningful changes that enhance their leadership style.

- Regular Self-Reflection: A leader's ability to assess past decisions, analyze interactions, and recognize behavioral patterns is crucial for personal and professional growth. Taking time to journal, reflect on meetings, and evaluate key decisions allows leaders to identify areas for improvement and recognize what strategies are working. Self-reflection encourages leaders to ask themselves, "What could I have done better?" "How did my actions affect my team?" and "What lessons can I take from this experience?" This habit fosters a mindset of continuous growth and self-improvement.

- Emotional Intelligence Training: Great leaders are not just intelligent—they are emotionally intelligent. Emotional intelligence (EI) plays a critical role in self-awareness, influencing how leaders manage emotions, navigate relationships, and make decisions. Developing skills in self-regulation, empathy, and social awareness helps leaders become more effective at handling conflict, building strong relationships, and understanding the needs of their teams. Investing in EI training, workshops, or assessments can significantly enhance a leader's ability to connect with others and foster a positive workplace culture.

- Executive Coaching or Mentorship: Leaders do not have to navigate their growth journey alone. Seeking guidance from experienced leaders, mentors, or professional coaches provides an opportunity for objective feedback, personal development strategies, and leadership insights. A mentor can help a leader gain perspective, challenge their assumptions, and offer valuable advice based on experience. Additionally, executive coaches use structured assessments and personalized strategies to help leaders refine their skills and reach their full potential.

Without self-awareness, leaders can become unintentionally destructive, making decisions that harm their teams and organizations while remaining blind to their own role in the dysfunction. Self-aware leaders, on the other hand, adapt, grow, and create environments where trust, collaboration, and innovation thrive. By implementing these tools and strategies, leaders can ensure they remain in touch with their strengths and weaknesses, continuously evolving to lead with integrity, empathy, and effectiveness.

Creating a Culture of Feedback and Continuous Improvement

One of the biggest mistakes failed leaders make is fearing feedback instead of embracing it. Leadership that rejects feedback creates stagnation, both for the leader's personal growth and for the organization as a whole. Great organizations thrive because they create open channels for constructive feedback, where employees feel safe to voice concerns, share ideas, and contribute to leadership development without fear of retaliation or dismissal.

A strong feedback culture allows organizations to identify weaknesses before they become major problems, adapt to changing needs, and continuously improve leadership effectiveness. When employees know their voices are valued and respected, they become more engaged, more innovative, and more invested in the company's success. Feedback should never be seen as a threat or a personal attack is a tool for growth, a pathway to self-awareness, and a cornerstone of strong leadership.

Developing Open Channels for Constructive Feedback

A culture of feedback does not happen by accident, it requires intentionality and structure. Organizations that encourage feedback create an open, transparent environment where leaders and employees collaborate to improve processes, communication, and workplace culture. Some effective ways to establish open channels of communication include:

- Regular One-on-One Meetings: Employees need dedicated time to share concerns, ask questions, and discuss their growth with leadership. Regular, structured conversations foster trust, engagement, and professional development.

- Anonymous Feedback Surveys: Some employees may hesitate to give honest feedback face-to-face due to fear of consequences. Anonymous surveys provide a safe way for employees to share concerns while ensuring that critical insights reach decision-makers.

- Leadership Office Hours or Open-Door Policies: Encouraging accessibility and approachability allows leaders to proactively invite dialogue rather than waiting for issues to escalate. When employees feel comfortable bringing concerns directly to leadership, trust and transparency grow.

- Feedback Training for Leaders: Receiving feedback is a skill. Leaders should be trained in how to listen, process, and act on feedback without becoming defensive. When leaders respond to feedback with an open mind and a commitment to improvement, it sets the tone for a culture of continuous learning and adaptation.

Organizations that fail to implement structured feedback systems create environments of frustration and disengagement. Employees who feel unheard or dismissed are far less likely to contribute ideas, innovate, or remain loyal to the company. The best organizations do not just collect feedback, they act on it.

Using Feedback as a Tool for Growth

Feedback is only valuable when it leads to action. Leaders who ignore or dismiss feedback create a stagnant workplace where employees stop trying to contribute. On the other hand, leaders who accept, internalize, and apply feedback build thriving organizations that continuously improve.

Leaders should view feedback as a tool for improvement rather than a form of criticism. It provides insight into leadership effectiveness, team morale, and workplace culture. Employees who see that their feedback leads to real change become more engaged, more motivated, and more committed to success.

The best leaders don't just hear feedback, they implement change. They recognize that leadership is a journey, not a destination, and that continuous learning and adaptation are the keys to long-term success. Organizations that foster a culture of learning, growth, and open communication build resilient teams and sustainable success.

Rebuilding Trust After Leadership Failures

Leadership mistakes are inevitable, no leader is perfect. However, what separates strong leaders from failed ones is how they respond to their missteps. Trust is one of the most fragile aspects of leadership—it can be lost in a moment but takes time and effort to rebuild.

Many leaders damage trust through poor decisions, unethical behavior, or failing to prioritize team well-being. While some leadership failures can be corrected, others, especially those rooted in dishonesty, manipulation, or repeated neglect, may be impossible to repair. However, in most cases, trust is not permanently lost, it can be restored through humility, transparency, and consistent action.

Leaders who take ownership of their mistakes and demonstrate genuine efforts to improve can gradually rebuild credibility and respect within their teams. The key is not just acknowledging failure but taking meaningful, sustained steps to correct it.

Steps to Regain Trust and Credibility

Rebuilding trust is a process, not an event. Leaders who have broken trust must take deliberate steps to prove they are committed to change. The following steps help restore confidence and repair damaged relationships within an organization:

- Acknowledge the Mistake Openly: Leaders must take full accountability rather than deflecting blame. Avoiding responsibility or making excuses only deepens the loss of trust.

Instead, leaders should own their mistakes and demonstrate that they understand the impact of their actions. Admitting failure is not a sign of weakness, it is a sign of integrity and self-awareness.

- Communicate the Steps for Change: Simply saying "I'm sorry" is not enough. Employees need to see a clear, actionable plan for improvement. Whether it involves adjusting leadership behavior, improving decision-making processes, or ensuring greater transparency, leaders must demonstrate commitment to meaningful change.

- Demonstrate Change Through Actions, Not Just Words: Trust is not rebuilt overnight; it is earned through consistent, positive behavior over time. Employees will only believe in leadership improvement if they see real, ongoing changes in how decisions are made, how communication is handled, and how teams are supported. Leaders must prove through daily actions that they are committed to being better.

- Invite Ongoing Feedback and Accountability: Leaders who are serious about regaining trust must allow their teams to hold them accountable. Regular check-ins, open discussions, and progress reports can show employees that leadership is taking feedback seriously and making tangible improvements.

Trust is not given, it is earned. It is built through honesty, integrity, and consistent follow-through. Leaders who have lost trust cannot demand it back; they must prove, through action, that they deserve it.

Final Thoughts on Trust and Leadership

Trust is the foundation of effective leadership. Without trust, communication breaks down, morale collapses, and teams become disengaged. A leader who has broken trust must be willing to put in the time, effort, and self-reflection necessary to rebuild it.

Leaders who respond to failure with denial, defensiveness, or avoidance will only deepen the disconnect with their teams. But leaders who face their failures head-on, communicate with transparency, and take meaningful action can restore credibility and create a stronger, more resilient organization.

At the end of the day, trust is not about being perfect, it's about being honest, accountable, and committed to continuous growth. The best leaders are not the ones who never make mistakes, but the ones who learn from them and come back stronger.

A Culture of Successful Leadership and How to Recognize Leadership Failures

A truly successful organization is not defined by a single great leader, it is built on a culture that continuously fosters strong leadership values at every level. When leadership development becomes ingrained in the organization's DNA, it ensures that future leaders are equipped, empowered, and held to high standards. Leadership should not be limited to a few individuals at the top, it should be a shared responsibility, where leaders are developed, mentored, and encouraged at every stage of an employee's career.

Organizations that prioritize a strong leadership culture do not rely on one charismatic figure to drive success; they create systems and structures that produce effective, ethical, and resilient leaders across all departments. This approach ensures that even if a key leader steps down, the company continues to thrive because the leadership pipeline is strong. Without this, companies become vulnerable to instability, inconsistency, and poor decision-making, allowing cycles of toxic leadership and organizational dysfunction to persist.

Key Traits of a Strong Leadership Culture

Organizations that cultivate great leaders do so by embedding key leadership values into their culture. They focus on mentorship, accountability, and transparent communication to ensure that leadership is not just a title but a responsibility. The following are hallmarks of a leadership-driven culture:

- Transparent Communication: Strong leadership starts with clarity and openness. Organizations that value transparency ensure that leaders and employees share information freely, keeping teams aligned with company goals. Open communication builds trust, fosters collaboration, and eliminates uncertainty, preventing the kind of secrecy that often fuels mistrust and disengagement.

- Mentorship and Leadership Development: Great leaders do not emerge by accident; they are trained, mentored, and given opportunities to develop. Successful organizations invest in leadership training programs to ensure that future leaders are prepared for their roles, not just promoted based on seniority or convenience. By fostering a culture where mentorship is a priority, organizations build a leadership pipeline that is ready to take on new challenges.

- Accountability for All Leaders: In a strong leadership culture, no one is above evaluation, criticism, or the need for improvement. Leaders are held to the same high standards as their teams, ensuring that power does not create ego-driven or unchecked decision-making. True leadership requires humility and accountability, and when leaders are open to feedback and growth, the entire organization benefits.

A strong leadership culture does not tolerate mediocrity or toxic behavior at the leadership level. It expects integrity, demands growth, and creates a workplace where leaders are developed, not just appointed.

Recognizing Leadership Failures Before They Do Damage

One of the most effective ways to prevent cycles of failed leadership is by identifying warning signs early. Leadership failures rarely happen overnight—they build up over time through neglect, arrogance, poor decision-making, or a refusal to adapt. Organizations that are proactive in assessing leadership effectiveness can intervene before small issues become catastrophic failures.

Some key red flags of ineffective or damaging leadership include:

- Leaders who resist feedback or dismiss concerns. When leaders are unwilling to listen, they create a culture of silence and disengagement. Employees stop voicing concerns, offering ideas, or contributing to problem-solving, leading to a slow deterioration of morale and innovation.

- A toxic work environment characterized by fear, favoritism, or low morale. Toxic leaders foster division, create instability, and prioritize personal loyalty over team success. Workplaces with high levels of stress, distrust, and unhealthy competition are often the result of poor leadership choices.

- High turnover rates due to leadership-related dissatisfaction. When employees consistently leave an organization citing issues with management, lack of growth opportunities, or workplace culture, leadership is often the root cause. Retaining talent is a hallmark of great leadership, while high turnover signals deep-seated problems.

- A lack of innovation or adaptability within the organization. Organizations led by rigid, outdated, or risk-averse leadership struggle to evolve. Leaders who refuse to embrace change, learn from mistakes, or listen to fresh ideas ultimately stagnate their organizations, making them vulnerable to competition and market shifts.

Recognizing these early warning signs allows organizations to course-correct before leadership failures derail progress, damage reputations, and drive away top talent.

Redefining Leadership for Long-Term Success

The cycle of failed leadership can only be broken when organizations prioritize self-awareness, feedback, trust, and leadership development. Leadership is not about titles, power, or authority; it is about serving, guiding, and creating an environment where people thrive. Organizations that fail to cultivate strong leadership values become stagnant, uninspired, and vulnerable to internal dysfunction.

Strong leadership is not accidental, it is cultivated, reinforced, and continuously improved. The best organizations do not tolerate poor leadership, they identify, correct, and replace ineffective leaders with those who act with integrity, humility, and purpose. They build a system where leadership is not a privilege, but a responsibility to the people and the organization.

At the heart of every great organization is a commitment to strong, ethical, and growth-oriented leadership. Leaders who are willing to grow, learn, and evolve set the standard for lasting success. Those who fail to adapt, ignore feedback, or resist accountability become part of the problem rather than the solution.

The question every leader should ask themselves is this: Are you willing to grow, learn, and evolve, or will you become part of the cycle of failed leadership? The choice defines not just your success, but the success of everyone you lead.

"Leadership isn't about perfection—it's about growth, accountability, and breaking cycles of failure through self-awareness, feedback, and action. True leaders don't fear feedback; they embrace it, using it as the cornerstone of continuous improvement and organizational success"

Chapter 11

Leadership Reimagined

Leadership is not a static concept; it is an evolving practice that must adapt to the changing needs of people, businesses, and society. Traditional leadership models, built on hierarchical control and rigid structures, no longer serve organizations in an era defined by rapid innovation, global challenges, and shifting workforce expectations. To thrive in the future, leaders must reimagine leadership, embracing new models that prioritize collaboration, empathy, adaptability, and authenticity.

This chapter explores the transformation from command-and-control leadership to collaborative models, the growing importance of leading with empathy and authenticity, and the challenges that future leaders must anticipate and prepare for. The leaders who succeed in the coming decades will not be those who cling to outdated methods, but those who embrace change, empower others, and redefine what it means to lead.

From Command-and-Control to Collaborative Leadership

For decades, leadership was largely defined by authority, hierarchy, and top-down control. Leaders were seen as decision-makers, enforcers, and supervisors, while employees were expected to follow orders without question. This command-and-control model, inspired in part by military leadership structures, worked well in industrial-age organizations, where efficiency, repetition, and discipline were prioritized over flexibility and innovation. However, in today's rapidly evolving, knowledge-driven economy, such rigid leadership approaches no longer work.

The Command-and-Control Model: Military vs. Corporate Leadership

In military operations, the command-and-control approach makes sense. Decisions often need to be made quickly and decisively, with clear chains of command ensuring order, discipline, and immediate execution. In combat or high-risk scenarios, hesitation, debate, or disobedience can mean the difference between life and death. Military leadership, while structured, is also built on trust, unit cohesion, and a deep commitment to mission success, which is why soldiers follow orders with precision and discipline.

However, the corporate world operates under entirely different circumstances. Business environments are not battlefields, and employees are not soldiers expected to execute commands without thought. While structure and accountability are still necessary, modern leadership requires flexibility, creativity, and collaboration. Unlike military settings where obedience is paramount, organizations that enforce rigid hierarchies and discourage independent thought risk:

- Alienating employees who want to contribute ideas, not just take orders.

- Stifling innovation by suppressing critical thinking and creative problem-solving.

- Creating disengaged teams who feel undervalued and powerless.

The corporate world thrives on adaptability, innovation, and empowerment, requiring leaders who facilitate and inspire rather than dictate and control. The workforce today expects involvement in decision-making, ownership of their work, and leaders who respect their expertise. The shift from command-and-control to collaborative leadership is not just a cultural change, it is a strategic necessity for long-term success.

Why Command-and-Control Leadership Fails in Modern Organizations

The business landscape has evolved significantly. Companies are no longer assembly lines where employees are expected to complete repetitive tasks with minimal deviation. Instead, organizations rely on knowledge workers, creative professionals, and highly skilled individuals who thrive in environments that foster autonomy and collaboration.

Leaders who cling to authoritarian, hierarchical structures often face the following challenges:

- Decreased Employee Engagement: Employees who feel like cogs in a machine, simply executing orders, often lose motivation and interest in their work. Engaged employees, on the other hand, feel valued and empowered because they have a voice in decision-making.

- Limited Innovation: Command-and-control leadership discourages independent thinking. When employees are not encouraged to share ideas, take risks, or challenge the status quo, companies fall behind competitors that embrace innovation and adaptability.

- High Turnover Rates: Talented employees do not stay in environments where they feel stifled, unheard, or micromanaged. Companies that fail to adapt their leadership models often struggle to retain top talent.

- Slow Decision-Making in Complex Situations: In today's fast-paced business world, decisions must be made quickly and collaboratively. Rigid, bureaucratic chains of command slow down problem-solving and prevent teams from responding to challenges effectively.

Traditional command-and-control leadership thrives in crisis situations where decisiveness and authority are necessary, but it fails in environments that require creativity, collaboration, and problem-solving. Ultimately, corporate America is not the military require two different leadership models.

The Shift to Team-Based Leadership Models

Collaborative leadership represents a fundamental departure from traditional hierarchical leadership structures. In a top-down model, power and decision-making rest with a small group of executives, while employees are expected to execute directives without questioning them. This approach limits creativity, slows decision-making, and prevents organizations from fully leveraging the skills and expertise of their workforce.

In contrast, team-based leadership models embrace shared responsibility, where decision-making is distributed across teams, departments, and individuals at all levels of the organization. Instead of a rigid chain of command, employees are actively involved in shaping strategies, solving problems, and driving company growth. This model creates a culture where employees feel a sense of ownership over their work, which leads to higher engagement, increased accountability, and better overall performance.

Key advantages of shifting to a team-based leadership model include:

- Encouraging Employees to Take Ownership: Employees who feel trusted and empowered take greater responsibility for their work. When people have a say in decisions that affect their roles, they are more invested in the outcomes. This results in higher motivation, stronger performance, and a greater willingness to innovate.

- Breaking Down Silos and Strengthening Collaboration: Many traditional organizations suffer from departmental silos, where teams operate in isolation, fail to communicate effectively, and

154

struggle with inefficiencies. A team-based leadership model ensures that different departments and functions work together toward shared goals, fostering cross-functional collaboration and seamless workflows.

- Boosting Innovation and Problem-Solving: When decision-making is decentralized, organizations benefit from a diverse range of perspectives, skill sets, and experiences. Employees at all levels—not just executives—can contribute insights, ideas, and creative solutions. This diversity of thought fuels innovation allows organizations to adapt more quickly and keeps them competitive in dynamic industries.

Some of the world's most successful companies have moved away from centralized leadership and embraced decentralized, team-based leadership models. Google, Pixar, and Spotify have implemented cross-functional teams, where employees are encouraged to contribute ideas, take initiative, and collaborate across different business areas. These companies trust their employees to lead projects, make key decisions, and drive innovation. The result? Higher job satisfaction, stronger employee retention, and groundbreaking innovations that continue to reshape industries.

The shift toward team-based leadership is not just about modernizing corporate culture, it is about building an organization that is more agile, more resilient, and better positioned for long-term success.

Shared Decision Making Empowers Employees

Many organizations hesitate to distribute decision-making power, fearing that too many voices will slow down processes or that employees may not make the "right" choices. However, research and real-world case studies consistently show that shared decision-making leads to stronger outcomes, better engagement, and increased adaptability.

The transition to collaborative leadership is not just about making employees feel good, it has measurable benefits that drive success at every level of an organization:

- Increased Agility and Adaptability: Organizations that rely on top-down decision-making often struggle to respond quickly to industry shifts, market disruptions, and global crises. When leadership is centralized, executives can become bottlenecks, delaying necessary changes. However, when decision-making is shared, teams can react faster, pivot strategies more effectively, and stay ahead of competitors.

- Higher Employee Engagement and Productivity: Employees who feel empowered and valued are more motivated, more committed, and more likely to go the extra mile. A study by Gallup found that employees who feel they have a voice in decision-making are significantly more engaged and more productive than those who feel disconnected from leadership.

- Stronger Innovation and Problem-Solving: When leaders encourage input from all levels of the organization, they unlock a greater range of ideas, experiences, and problem-solving skills. Innovation is no longer dependent on a small leadership team; it becomes a core part of company culture.

When employees are actively involved in decision-making, they are not just workers executing orders, they are problem-solvers, innovators, and contributors to the company's future. This shift not only makes organizations more effective, but it also builds a workforce that is deeply invested in long-term success.

The future of leadership is not about control, it is about enabling and empowering others to succeed. Organizations that embrace this philosophy will outperform those that cling to outdated, hierarchical leadership models.

Leading with Empathy and Authenticity

In today's workplace, leadership is no longer just about strategy, execution, and results—it is about building meaningful relationships, fostering trust, and creating an environment where employees feel valued, heard, and supported. Employees do not just want a boss; they want a leader who understands them as human beings. However, empathy must be balanced with accountability, understanding an employee's struggles is important but so is ensuring that they meet performance expectations and fulfill their responsibilities.

How Empathy Transforms Leadership

Empathetic leaders recognize the challenges, emotions, and aspirations of their teams. They listen actively, seek to understand different perspectives, and make decisions that consider both business objectives and employee well-being. When leaders show empathy, employees feel safer, more engaged, and more motivated to contribute.

However, empathy does not mean lowering standards or accepting poor performance. A leader's role is to support employees while also holding them accountable for their work. Compassion and expectations must go hand in hand, leaders who lean too far into empathy without maintaining accountability risk fostering complacency, while those who focus solely on performance without consideration for employee well-being create a toxic culture of burnout.

A culture of balanced empathy in leadership leads to:

- Higher Employee Retention: Employees are far more likely to stay with a company where they feel valued, respected, and supported. Companies with empathetic leadership experience lower turnover and greater employee loyalty. However, employees also want structure and clear expectations—if a workplace is too lenient, high performers may become frustrated by a lack of accountability among their peers.

- Improved Team Morale and Collaboration: Teams work better when they feel psychologically safe, but that does not mean eliminating accountability. When leaders show understanding and compassion, employees are more willing to collaborate, take risks, and support each other's success, if everyone is contributing equally and fairly.

- Increased Performance and Motivation: Employees perform at their best when they feel appreciated, but appreciation must be paired with high expectations. Leaders who listen, mentor, and guide their teams while still enforcing standards see higher levels of productivity, creativity, and commitment.

Balancing Empathy with Accountability

Empathy does not mean excusing poor performance, overlooking missed deadlines, or allowing employees to underdeliver. Instead, it means recognizing struggles, providing support, and ensuring that employees have the tools and resources they need to succeed—but also holding them accountable for meeting expectations.

A truly effective leader understands that:

- Compassion Must Come with Clarity: Leaders should acknowledge employee struggles but also set clear expectations about job performance. If an employee is falling behind, an empathetic leader does not ignore the problem—they address constructively, offering solutions, guidance, and support.
- Flexibility Does Not Mean a Free Pass: Life happens, illness, family emergencies, and mental health struggles are real, and leaders must be understood. However, chronic underperformance without effort to improve is a different issue. Empathy means helping employees overcome obstacles, not excusing avoidable failures.

- Tough Conversations Are Still Necessary: Holding employees accountable does not have to be harsh or punitive—but it does have to be direct and honest. Leaders must be willing to have difficult conversations, offering both encouragement and constructive criticism.

Empathy Without Accountability Leads to Dysfunction

The best leaders are both compassionate and firm. They build relationships, foster trust, and care about their teams, but they also expect results, demand accountability, and ensure that everyone is pulling their weight. Empathy without accountability creates complacency, while accountability without empathy breeds resentment—true leadership lies in balancing both effectively.

Leaders who master this balance create workplaces that are both supportive and high performing, where employees feel valued, challenged, and motivated to succeed.

How Genuine Connections Drive Loyalty and Performance

Empathetic leaders recognize that people are not just workers, they are individuals with emotions, challenges, and aspirations. When leadership focuses only on output and productivity without considering the human aspect of work, employees become disengaged, unmotivated, and more likely to leave. However, when leaders prioritize connection and understanding, they cultivate a workplace culture where employees feel valued, respected, and genuinely invested in the success of the organization.

By fostering genuine connections, leaders can dramatically improve retention, morale, and overall performance. The benefits include:

- Higher Employee Retention: People are far more likely to stay with companies where they feel respected and supported. Employees who feel disconnected or undervalued will look elsewhere for opportunities where they feel their contributions matter. Companies that build strong relationships with their employees create loyalty, reducing turnover costs and retaining top talent.

- Improved Team Morale and Collaboration: Trust is the foundation of effective teamwork. When employees trust their leaders and believe their best interests are considered, they are more likely to collaborate, share ideas, and support one another. A workplace culture built on genuine relationships and trust leads to stronger team cohesion and greater collective success.

- Increased Performance and Motivation: Employees perform at their best when they feel valued, heard, and appreciated. Leaders who actively listen, provide recognition, and engage with their teams on a personal level inspire higher levels of commitment, creativity, and productivity. When people feel like their work matters, they put in extra effort and take pride in their contributions.

A study published by Harvard Business Review found that leaders who demonstrate emotional intelligence and empathy are significantly more effective at engaging employees, driving performance, and reducing workplace stress. Empathy is not just a "soft" leadership skill, it is a strategic advantage that fosters resilience, loyalty, and long-term success.

Strategies for Building Trust Through Vulnerability and Honest Communication

One of the most powerful leadership tools is authenticity. Employees do not expect leaders to be perfect—but they do expect them to be real. When leaders hide behind authority, avoid difficult conversations, or refuse to acknowledge mistakes, they create a disconnect between themselves and their teams. However, when they embrace transparency, show vulnerability, and communicate openly, they foster a culture of trust and engagement.

Here are key strategies for building trust through honesty and vulnerability:

- Admit When You Don't Have All the Answers: Strong leaders do not pretend to know everything. Instead, they involve their teams in problem-solving and seek input from others. Admitting uncertainty and collaborating on solutions creates a stronger sense of ownership among employees.

- Be Transparent About Challenges and Setbacks: Leadership is not about maintaining a flawless image, it is about navigating difficulties with integrity. Instead of hiding mistakes or failures, authentic leaders address them openly, explain the lessons learned, and focus on actionable solutions. Employees respect leaders who tell the truth, even when it's difficult.

- Show Vulnerability: Leaders who are willing to be vulnerable, whether by admitting past mistakes, sharing a personal struggle, or acknowledging their limitations, create deeper connections with their teams. Vulnerability humanizes leaders, making them more relatable and trustworthy.

Authenticity, empathy, and open communication are not signs of weakness, they are leadership superpowers that drive engagement, loyalty, and innovation. The more leaders embrace these principles, the stronger their organizations will be.

Preparing for Emerging Challenges

The future of leadership will be more complex, fast-paced, and unpredictable than ever before. The leaders who thrive in the coming decades will be those who can adapt, innovate, and anticipate new challenges before they arise. Leadership is no longer just about managing operations and driving results, it is about navigating uncertainty, inspiring resilience, and shaping the future of work.

Key Challenges Future Leaders Must Prepare For:

- AI Integration and Workplace Automation: The rise of artificial intelligence and automation will reshape industries, job roles, and workplace dynamics. Leaders must balance the adoption of technology with ethical considerations, ensuring that automation enhances productivity without dehumanizing the workforce. Workforce reskilling and human-centric leadership will be critical in preparing teams for the future.

- Global Crises and Economic Uncertainty: From pandemics to climate change to geopolitical tensions, the world will continue to face unprecedented challenges. Effective leaders will need to make tough decisions under pressure, navigate uncertainty, and inspire resilience in their teams. The ability to lead through crises with clarity and composure will define the next generation of leadership.

- Shifting Workforce Expectations: As Gen Z and younger generations enter the workforce, leadership will need to adapt to evolving expectations around work-life balance, remote flexibility, and purpose-driven careers. Younger employees seek meaning, autonomy, and companies that align with their values. Organizations that fail to evolve with these changing expectations will struggle to attract and retain top talent.

The future belongs to leaders who embrace change, prioritize people, and lead with vision and adaptability.

Case Studies: Organizations That Successfully Navigated Leadership Transformations

Some of the most successful companies today were able to pivot, embrace change, and redefine leadership models to thrive in the modern business landscape. These companies prove that bold leadership decisions can drive lasting impact:

- Netflix's Transformation from DVDs to Streaming: Netflix successfully pivoted from a DVD rental business to a global digital streaming giant by embracing agility, innovation, and decentralized decision-making. Instead of resisting change, Netflix led the industry forward, transforming how people consume entertainment.

- Microsoft's Leadership Shift Under Satya Nadella: Microsoft, once rigid and hierarchical, transformed into a collaborative, growth-oriented organization under CEO Satya Nadella. He prioritized innovation, empathy, and purpose-driven leadership, shifting the company's culture to one of continuous learning and adaptability.

- Patagonia's Purpose-Driven Leadership: Patagonia integrated social and environmental responsibility into its business model, proving that profit and purpose can coexist. The company's leadership prioritizes sustainability, ethical production, and activism, creating a strong brand identity and loyal customer base.

These companies embraced change, empowered their employees, and redefined leadership, positioning themselves as industry leaders in their respective fields.

Leaders of Tomorrow

Leadership is being redefined. The future will not belong to those who cling to authority, resist feedback, or lead through fear will belong to those who collaborate, empower, and lead with empathy and authenticity.

The leaders who embrace transformation, prioritize human connection, and adapt to new challenges will build organizations that thrive in the decades to come. They will lead not by dictating but by inspiring, fostering cultures of trust, adaptability, and innovation.

"Leadership is no longer about commanding from the top—it's about empowering from within. By shifting from control to collaboration, leaders foster innovation, resilience, and a culture where every voice drives success"

Chapter 12

The Leadership Legacy

Managing people and leadership are two different things. Nor is it about achieving quarterly goals or climbing the corporate ladder. True leadership is about impact—on individuals, organizations, and even society as a whole. The leaders who leave a lasting legacy are not those who seek personal recognition, but those who inspire, empower, and cultivate growth in others.

This final chapter reflects on the core lessons of effective leadership, the importance of continuous self-improvement, and how leaders can extend their influence beyond their immediate roles to create meaningful, lasting change. Leadership is not just a title, it's a responsibility to shape the future.

Recap of Key Lessons

Throughout this book, we have explored the qualities, strategies, and challenges that define impactful leadership. Successful leaders are not defined by power, status, or authority, they are defined by their ability to communicate, connect, adapt, and inspire.

The Core Elements of Effective Leadership

Effective leadership is built on a foundation of vision, emotional intelligence, trust, accountability, and adaptability. Great leaders do not just manage tasks, they inspire people, drive progress, and create a culture of success.

Vision and Clear Communication

Leadership begins with a compelling vision and the ability to communicate it effectively. Without clarity, teams become directionless, disengaged, and ineffective. The best leaders paint a clear picture of success, ensuring that everyone understands not just what they are working toward, but why it matters. A well-communicated vision provides purpose and motivation, aligning employees toward a shared goal and creating a sense of collective mission.

Emotional Intelligence and Trust Building

The strongest leaders are not just strategically intelligent, they are emotionally intelligent. Leadership is not about authority, it is about influence, and influence is built on trust, empathy, and authenticity. Leaders who prioritize emotional intelligence create an environment where employees feel valued, heard, and supported. They understand that psychological safety is critical to high performance, allowing teams to collaborate, take risks, and innovate without fear. Trust is the currency of leadership, and those who cultivate it foster loyalty, engagement, and long-term success.

Accountability and Adaptability

Leadership is not about being perfect, it is about being responsible. Great leaders own their mistakes, learn from feedback, and continuously refine their approach. They recognize that growth comes from challenges, and instead of fearing failure or uncertainty, they embrace them as opportunities for improvement. Adaptability is essential in today's fast-changing world—leaders who resist change fall behind, while those who are open to learning and evolving thrive. Accountability ensures integrity and credibility, reinforcing that leaders must lead by example and hold themselves to the same high standards as their teams.

Together, these elements form the foundation of impactful leadership. Leaders who embrace vision, emotional intelligence, trust, accountability, and adaptability create stronger teams, better workplaces, and lasting success.

Consequences of Poor Leadership vs. Benefits of Getting It Right

Leadership is one of the greatest determining factors in the success or failure of an organization. Poor leadership has far-reaching consequences, negatively impacting morale, performance, innovation, and overall organizational health. A workplace led by ineffective leadership suffers from high employee turnover, disengagement, and dysfunction. When employees feel undervalued, unheard, or micromanaged, they either underperform or leave for better opportunities, causing instability and loss of talent. Poor leadership destroys trust, creates toxic work environments, and limits progress by stifling creativity and collaboration.

In contrast, great leadership is transformative. It fosters engagement, drives productivity, and builds thriving cultures where people feel valued, motivated, and inspired to perform at their best. Leaders who exhibit vision, emotional intelligence, and accountability create an environment where trust and respect are foundational, leading to higher job satisfaction, stronger teamwork, and long-term success. Companies led by visionary, emotionally intelligent, and adaptable leaders experience greater longevity, resilience, and innovation, positioning themselves as industry leaders.

Leadership is not just about short-term wins, it is about building something meaningful that outlasts you. A leader's true legacy is not measured by profits or titles but by the lasting impact they have on the people and organizations they serve. Those who lead with integrity, empathy, and accountability ensure that their influence continues to inspire and create success long after their tenure ends.

The Importance of Continuous Growth

Leadership is not a destination, it is a lifelong journey of learning, reflection, and self-improvement. The most effective leaders never believe they have 'arrived' or that they know everything there is to know. Instead, they are constantly seeking opportunities to grow, challenge themselves, and evolve with changing times. Great leadership is not about achieving a title, it is about maintaining a mindset of curiosity, adaptability, and resilience.

Committing to Lifelong Learning

One of the defining characteristics of exceptional leaders is their commitment to continuous growth. They understand that leadership is not static—it requires ongoing development and self-awareness. To cultivate this growth, leaders must:

- Seek Feedback: The best leaders actively seek input from their teams, peers, and mentors. They listen without defensiveness, viewing feedback as a tool for improvement rather than a personal attack. Leaders who embrace constructive criticism refine their skills, improve decision-making, and build stronger relationships with their teams.

- Embrace Challenges: Every leadership challenge is an opportunity for growth. Leaders who lean into adversity rather than avoiding it develop resilience, creativity, and problem-solving skills. Challenges test a leader's ability to adapt and innovate, ultimately strengthening their leadership capabilities.

- Stay Open to Change: The world is constantly evolving, and great leaders evolve with it. They do not cling to outdated practices or resist new ideas—they adapt, innovate, and embrace change as an essential part of leadership. Those who fail to change risk becoming obsolete, while those who remain open-minded and forward-thinking continue to lead effectively.

168

Leadership excellence is not about knowing everything, it is about continuously striving to learn more. Leaders who commit to lifelong learning create organizations that thrive, innovate, and stay ahead of the curve. The best leaders are not just learners themselves, they inspire learning in others, creating a culture of continuous growth and improvement.

Leaving a Lasting Impact

The greatest leaders do not measure their success by personal achievements alone, they measure it by the success of those they inspire and develop. True leadership is not about individual accomplishments; it is about collective progress and long-term impact. A leader's legacy is not defined by how high they rise but by how many others they lift along the way.

Inspiring Others and Fostering a Culture of Growth

Great leaders elevate those around them, creating environments where people feel empowered, supported, and encouraged to reach their full potential. They understand that their role is not to command, but to cultivate talent and build strong, capable teams.

To foster a culture of growth, great leaders:

- Mentor and Develop Future Leaders: They invest time, energy, and resources into coaching others, ensuring that leadership does not end with them. They share their knowledge and experiences, helping others navigate challenges and grow into leadership roles.

- Encourage Innovation and Independent Thinking: Instead of micromanaging, they trust their teams, giving them the autonomy to take initiative and contribute ideas. When employees feel empowered to think independently and solve problems creatively, organizations thrive on innovation rather than stagnating in routine.

- Recognize and Celebrate Achievements: They acknowledge the contributions of others, ensuring that team members feel valued, motivated, and engaged. A culture of recognition fosters a positive work environment, where employees are more committed, more productive, and more willing to go the extra mile.

The best leaders understand that success is not about personal recognition, it is about creating a team of confident, capable individuals who drive progress together.

Building a Leadership Pipeline

For organizations to thrive long-term, leadership must be sustainable. When leaders fail to cultivate new leaders, organizations become overly dependent on a single figure, making them vulnerable to collapse when that leader steps down.

The best leaders recognize that their greatest achievement is not what they build, it is who they develop. They identify potential in others, provide growth opportunities, and prepare successors to carry the vision forward. A strong leadership pipeline ensures that organizations remain stable, innovative, and successful for years to come.

True leadership is not about creating a personal legacy, it is about ensuring the continued success of those who follow. The leaders who prioritize mentorship, talent development, and knowledge-sharing leave behind something far greater than a title, they leave behind a lasting impact that extends beyond their own tenure.

Leadership Beyond the Organization

Great leadership does not stop at the workplace. The most impactful leaders use their influence to drive positive change in society, advocate for important causes, and inspire transformation beyond their teams and organizations.

Leadership at its highest level is about creating a better world, whether through business ethics, social responsibility, sustainability, or community engagement. Many of history's most influential leaders have gone beyond their professional roles to drive wider societal impact.

Leaders who understand their broader responsibility do not just run businesses or manage teams; they stand for something greater, leaving behind a legacy of positive change that extends well beyond their immediate sphere of influence.

True leadership is not just about career success, it is about making a meaningful difference in the lives of others, within organizations, and in the world at large.

Driving Positive Societal, Environmental, and Ethical Change

Leadership extends far beyond the workplace. The most influential leaders understand their responsibility to create positive change, not just within their organizations but in society as a whole. Whether through corporate social responsibility, environmental sustainability, or ethical leadership, great leaders set an example that transcends business success and drives meaningful progress in the world.

Today's consumers, employees, and stakeholders expect more from leaders. It is no longer enough to focus solely on profits, modern leadership demands a commitment to broader ethical, social, and environmental issues. Organizations that prioritize sustainability, diversity, and corporate responsibility not only gain trust and loyalty but also position themselves as forward-thinking industry leaders.

Some of the most impactful leaders in history have used their influence to drive positive change, proving that leadership is not just about managing business, it is about shaping a better future.

Examples of Leaders Who Made a Broader Impact

- Paul Polman (Unilever): As the former CEO of Unilever, Polman transformed the company into a sustainability-driven organization, proving that business success and ethical responsibility can go hand in hand. Under his leadership, Unilever prioritized environmental impact, sustainable sourcing, and fair labor practices, setting a standard for corporations worldwide.

- Yvon Chouinard (Patagonia): The founder of Patagonia built a business model rooted in environmental conservation, demonstrating that companies can be both profitable and purpose driven. Patagonia's leadership philosophy prioritizes sustainability, ethical production, and activism, proving that business can be a force for good without sacrificing success.

- Oprah Winfrey: Using her platform to inspire, educate, and advocate for social change, Oprah has shown that leadership extends beyond business into cultural impact. Through philanthropy, education initiatives, and public advocacy, she has empowered millions and proven that influence should be used to uplift others.

Great leadership is not confined to boardrooms, it has the potential to shape industries, communities, and future generations. The most memorable leaders are not those who simply accumulate wealth or power, but those who leave the world better than they find it.

Lead with Purpose

Leadership is not about status, it is about service. True leaders do not seek power for personal gain, they take responsibility, make bold decisions, and inspire others to rise to their full potential. They leave a legacy, not by holding on to authority, but by empowering those around them to succeed.

The Challenge: Will You Lead with Integrity, Vision, and Empathy?

- Will you be a leader who listens, learns, and grows?

- Will you inspire those around you to achieve more than they thought possible?

- Will you build something meaningful that lasts beyond your tenure?

The choice is yours. The future of leadership is being written right now—and those who lead with purpose, authenticity, and vision will shape what comes next.

Leadership is not about being in charge, it is about making a difference. What difference will you make?

Leadership Challenges That Lie Ahead

Leadership is not just about making decisions, it is about making a difference. It is about leaving something greater than yourself, a team that thrives, an organization that evolves, a legacy that outlasts your tenure.

The most influential leaders do not cling to power; they use their influence to empower others. They do not hoard success; they share it generously. They do not resist change; they embrace it as a force for growth and transformation.

Leadership is not about authority; it is about responsibility. It is about having the courage to make tough choices, the humility to admit mistakes, and the vision to see what others cannot yet imagine. It is about lifting others, not standing above them.

Here's the truth: The world does not need more managers who simply enforce rules—it needs leaders who inspire change. Leaders who are willing to challenge the status quo, take risks, and stand for something bigger than themselves. Leaders who cultivate trust, build people up, and create a ripple effect of leadership beyond their own sphere of influence.

Finally, ask yourself:

- What kind of leader will you be?

- Will you lead with purpose, integrity, and vision?

- Will you be the leader who empowers others to lead?

Because in the end, the true measure of leadership is not how many followers you have, it is how many leaders you create.

"A true leader's legacy is not defined by their personal accomplishments, but by the people they inspire, the growth they cultivate, and the lasting impact they leave behind on organizations, communities, and society as a whole"

Bibliography

Antonakis, J., & House, R. J. (2014). Instrumental leadership: Measurement and extension of transformational–transactional leadership theory. The Leadership Quarterly, 25(4), 746–771. https://doi.org/10.1016/j.leaqua.2014.04.005

Avolio, B. J., & Gardner, W. L. (2005). Authentic leadership development: Getting to the root of positive forms of leadership. The Leadership Quarterly, 16(3), 315–338. https://doi.org/10.1016/j.leaqua.2005.03.001

Avolio, B. J., Walumbwa, F. O., & Weber, T. J. (2009). Leadership: Current theories, research, and future directions. Annual Review of Psychology, 60, 421–449. https://doi.org/10.1146/annurev.psych.60.110707.163621

Bass, B. M. (1999). Two decades of research and development in transformational leadership. European Journal of Work and Organizational Psychology, 8(1), 9–32. https://doi.org/10.1080/135943299398410

Blake, R. R., & Mouton, J. S. (1964). The managerial grid. Gulf Publishing.

Burns, J. M. (1978). Leadership. Harper & Row.

Day, D. V., Fleenor, J. W., Atwater, L. E., Sturm, R. E., & McKee, R. A. (2014). Advances in leader and leadership development: A review of 25 years of research and theory. The Leadership Quarterly, 25(1), 63–82. https://doi.org/10.1016/j.leaqua.2013.11.004

Dinh, J. E., Lord, R. G., Gardner, W. L., Meuser, J. D., Liden, R. C., & Hu, J. (2014). Leadership theory and research in the new millennium: Current theoretical trends and changing perspectives. The Leadership Quarterly, 25(1), 36–62. https://doi.org/10.1016/j.leaqua.2013.11.005

Eagly, A. H., & Carli, L. L. (2007). Women and the labyrinth of leadership. Harvard Business Review, 85(9), 62–71.

Fiedler, F. E. (1967). A theory of leadership effectiveness. McGraw-Hill.

Gabelica, C., Van den Bossche, P., Segers, M., & Gijselaers, W. (2012). Feedback, a powerful lever in teams: A review. Educational Research Review, 7(2), 123–144. https://doi.org/10.1016/j.edurev.2011.11.003

Goleman, D. (2000). Leadership that gets results. Harvard Business Review, 78(2), 78–90.

Graen, G. B., & Uhl-Bien, M. (1995). Relationship-based approach to leadership: Development of leader-member exchange (LMX) theory of leadership over 25 years: Applying a multi-level multi-domain perspective. The Leadership Quarterly, 6(2), 219–247. https://doi.org/10.1016/1048-9843(95)90036-5

Heifetz, R. A. (1994). Leadership without easy answers. Harvard University Press.

Hoch, J. E., & Dulebohn, J. H. (2013). Shared leadership in enterprise resource planning and human resource management system implementation. Human Resource Management Review, 23(1), 114–125. https://doi.org/10.1016/j.hrmr.2012.06.007

Hogan, R., & Kaiser, R. B. (2005). What we know about leadership. Review of General Psychology, 9(2), 169–180. https://doi.org/10.1037/1089-2680.9.2.169

House, R. J. (1971). A path goal theory of leader effectiveness. Administrative Science Quarterly, 16(3), 321–339. https://doi.org/10.2307/2391905

Judge, T. A., & Piccolo, R. F. (2004). Transformational and transactional leadership: A meta-analytic test of their relative validity. Journal of Applied Psychology, 89(5), 755–768. https://doi.org/10.1037/0021-9010.89.5.755

Katz, D., & Kahn, R. L. (1978). The social psychology of organizations (2nd ed.). Wiley.

Kouzes, J. M., & Posner, B. Z. (2011). The five practices of exemplary leadership. Pfeiffer.

Mazzetti, G., & Schaufeli, W. B. (2022). The impact of engaging leadership on employee engagement and team effectiveness: A longitudinal, multi-level study on the mediating role of personal- and team resources. PLOS ONE, 17(6), e0269745. https://doi.org/10.1371/journal.pone.0269745

Mintzberg, H. (1973). The nature of managerial work. Harper & Row.

Northouse, P. G. (2018). Leadership: Theory and practice (8th ed.). Sage Publications.

Stogdill, R. M. (1948). Personal factors associated with leadership: A survey of the literature. Journal of Psychology, 25(1), 35–71. https://doi.org/10.1080/00223980.1948.9917362

Tannenbaum, R., & Schmidt, W. H. (1958). How to choose a leadership pattern. Harvard Business Review, 36(2), 95–101.

Uhl-Bien, M., Marion, R., & McKelvey, B. (2007). Complexity leadership theory: Shifting leadership from the industrial age to the knowledge era. The Leadership Quarterly, 18(4), 298–318. https://doi.org/10.1016/j.leaqua.2007.04.002

Vroom, V. H., & Yetton, P. W. (1973). Leadership and decision-making. University of Pittsburgh Press.

Yukl, G. (2012). Effective leadership behavior: What we know and what questions need more attention. Academy of Management Perspectives, 26(4), 66–85. https://doi.org/10.5465/amp.2012.0088

About the author

Douglas B. Sims, PhD, is a visionary leader and environmental soil scientist with over three decades of professional experience. As a serial entrepreneur, Dr. Sims founded, grew, and successfully sold five startup companies in the environmental consulting industry, building a reputation for leadership, innovation, and business acumen. In 2011, he transitioned to higher education, bringing his entrepreneurial mindset and expertise into academia. Over the past 14 years, Dr. Sims has advanced student success and workforce development, serving as an environmental science instructor and later as the Dean of the School of Science, Engineering, and Mathematics at a leading Nevada college.

Dr. Sims' work is widely published in peer-reviewed journals, reflecting his commitment to advancing knowledge in his field. His leadership experience spans the corporate and academic worlds, giving him unique insights into the dynamics of organizational growth, management, and team building. He is passionate about the intersection of human behavior, leadership strategy, and sustainable development.

Married to his college sweetheart since the early 1990s, Dr. Sims and his wife have raised two grown children and instilled in them the values of hard work and lifelong learning. With a rich background that bridges industry and academia, Dr. Sims offers a compelling perspective on leadership, drawing from his journey of leading startups to success and shaping the next generation of leaders in higher education.